ADVANCE PRAISE

"Better than anyone else, Mardy Grothe uses classical quotations from history to share the powerful insights they can provide. In *Deconstructing Trump,* he builds a quotational congress of world voices spanning over two millennia, deftly showing how Donald Trump's actions run counter to history's desire to make the world a better place. Grothe gives us an illuminating understanding through collective historical wisdom."

JOHN BUSBEE, *The Culture Buzz*

"Mardy Grothe's thought-provoking new book *Deconstructing Trump* is a collection of a thousand points of light. These prescient historical quotations shine brightly on the hollowness of the man they so clearly bring to mind. When the history of The Trump Era is written, Grothe's name will be among those who chose to speak up.

ANU GARG, founder of Wordsmith.org and author of *A Word A Day*

"*Deconstructing Trump* is a brilliant idea consummately executed! Only a quotation maven with a scholar's grasp of intellectual history could produce this incredible foretelling of Trump. With a gentle hand on the reader's shoulder, Grothe provides a guided tour through centuries of astonishingly prescient quotations. *Deconstructing Trump* corroborates what our eyes and ears can scarcely believe. For some, it will be a comforting reminder that, like other dark periods in history, this too shall pass. I cannot imagine someone buying the book without picking up a gift copy or two for like-minded friends."

ROSALIE MAGGIO, bestselling author of *How to Say It*

"With so many salient quotes to reflect on, it was hard to choose which one best 'deconstructed' the subject of this hard-hitting collection. The Introduction hits the core message in a solid way and comments throughout greatly add to the reader's understanding. Indeed, the whole book reads like a gold-mine of historical insight brought into the present. Here's my favorite quote: 'Those who never retract their opinions love themselves more than they love truth.' (Joseph Joubert) Congrats to Dr. Mardy for this masterful collection."

BARBARA MCNICHOL, Editor and creator of *Word Trippers*

"If you are in despair at the way the world has incontestably taken a turn for the worse since the rise of Trump and his ilk, you may find a modicum of solace in Mardy Grothe's excellent new collection. To know that history has grappled with the problem before our time and has discussed it in highly quotable terms, may just about help us to win through."

NIGEL REES, British quotation scholar and legendary host of "Quote...Unquote"

"This is a wonderful book—erudite, passionate, and, most of all, heartening because it reminds us that narcissistic and bullying leaders have been with us all through history, and that people of wisdom, from Aristotle to Frank Zappa, have always seen through their lies and posturing, and thereby limited the damage they can do."

LAURENCE SHAMES, bestselling author of the Key West Capers series and other books

We live in a time when seemingly all of our democratic institutions and values are imperiled by kakistocracy—that is, government by the worst leaders. Mardy Grothe, our most popular and entertaining quotation collector, brings his formidable talents to bear on assembling fascinating quotes from history that read uncannily like descriptions of the present situation. All those who cherish the things that truly make America great will be gratified and inspired by the fruits of Grothe's brilliant labors.

FRED SHAPIRO, Editor of *The Yale Book of Quotations*

Also by Mardy Grothe

Metaphors Be With You (2016)

Neverisms (2011)

Ifferisms (2009)

I Never Metaphor I Didn't Like (2008)

Viva la Repartee (2005)

Oxymoronica (2004)

Never Let a Fool Kiss You or a Kiss Fool You (1999)

DECONSTRUCTING TRUMP

**The Trump Phenomenon Through
the Lens of Quotation History**

Dr. Mardy Grothe

Quoterie Press
Pinehurst, North Carolina

Deconstructing Trump: The Trump Phenomenon
Through the Lens of Quotation History
© 2019, Dr. Mardy Grothe. All Rights Reserved.
Published by Quoterie Press, Pinehurst, North Carolina

978-1-7332850-0-1 (paperback)
978-1-7332850-1-8 (eBook)
Library of Congress Control Number: 2019910844

https://deconstructingtrump.com/
@deconstructingtrump (Instagram)

Publishing consultant: David Wogahn
AuthorImprints.com

DEDICATION

To Donald J. Trump, without whose assistance
this book would not have been necessary.

CONTENTS

A PERSONAL NOTE
TO THE READER

In Book IV of his *Laws*, written in the 4th c. BC, Plato wrote:

**There is simple ignorance, which is
the source of lighter offenses,
and double ignorance, which is
accompanied by a conceit of wisdom;
and he who is under the influence of the latter fancies that
he knows all about matters of which he knows nothing.**

If your first thought was, "That sounds a lot like Donald Trump!" then you and I are on a similar wavelength. So sit back, relax, and get ready for what I hope will be an enjoyable and stimulating ride (or, more precisely, an enjoyable and stimulating *read*).

If, however, your first thought was, "That sounds a lot like Barack Obama!" then you and I are on different wavelengths. But if Barack Obama *is* your honest answer, do you remember how you felt in the days immediately after John McCain was defeated by Obama in the 2008 presidential election?

Do you recall how disappointed and even despondent you felt when McCain went down to defeat? Do you recall how angry you were at your fellow Republicans who switched sides and voted the Democratic ticket? Do you recall your confusion—even bewilderment—at how a relatively unknown political figure could defeat an experienced national leader with a reputation for honor and integrity? And, finally, do you recall how foreboding the future seemed at that moment, and how anxious you felt about life in America—especially *your* life—during an Obama presidency?

If you can recall those feelings, then we have something in common—for that is exactly how I felt after the 2016 presidential election.

In my experience, when people have something in common, they can have a fruitful dialogue even when they fundamentally disagree on politics, religion, or other matters. So, please, feel free to come along for the ride. You may not find it as enjoyable as my left-leaning friends, but I believe you will find it equally stimulating.

INTRODUCTION

Word and language lovers have long known that centuries-old sayings can have great relevance to present-day issues and problems. This book is a compilation of 1,000 quotations from the past—most from the *very* distant past—that speak to the ascendancy of an unconventional, controversial, and even clownish political novice, Donald J. Trump, to the presidency of the United States of America.

Not a single featured quotation in this anthology comes from the current century, and none mention Trump by name. *All of them* come from people writing many decades—or, more typically, many centuries—before the so-called Trump Era. As I was compiling the quotations, I considered writing an article titled "What Would Confucius (and Other Ancient Thinkers) Think of Trump?" but it never got written. A similar fate happened to articles with similar titles, including "What Would Ben Franklin (and Other Founding Fathers) Think of Trump?" and "What Would Shakespeare (and Other Great Writers) Think of Trump?" While these articles never got written, they may give you a better idea of what you'll find in these pages.

How This Book Came About

Like many millions of Americans, I was taken aback when, in the heat of the 2015 presidential primary season, an upstart candidate for the Republican Party's nomination questioned the heroic status of Arizona Senator John McCain. I'm sure you remember the moment.

In a July 2015 presidential forum at the Family Leadership Summit in Ames, Iowa, Donald J. Trump told interviewer Frank Luntz that he had supported McCain for president in the 2008 presidential election, and even donated generously to his campaign. Trump then went on to say: "I supported him. He lost. He let us down. But he lost, so I never liked him so much after that, because I don't like losers." After Luntz interjected, "But he's a war hero," Trump clearly said, "He's not a war hero." Before a stunned crowd, Luntz interjected again, this time to say that McCain had spent five-and-a-half years in a North Vietnamese prison camp. Trump replied smugly:

He was a war hero because he was captured.
I like people who weren't captured.

The crowd was clearly displeased with Trump's remarks and, at the time, it seemed like a stupid and self-defeating thing to say. Why, after all, would a man seeking the Republican presidential nomination besmirch a GOP icon before an audience of the Party's faithful?

I was surprised by Trump's remark, but not particularly shocked, for he was notorious for behaving in outrageous and offensive ways. Whenever he disagreed with people, he frequently went out of his way to bad-mouth them—often in a stunningly insulting manner. And even worse than his McCain remarks, from my perspective, were his years of false—and scurrilous—charges about Barack Obama's being born in Kenya, and therefore ineligible to serve as the US president.

As a long-time admirer of both McCain and Obama, it was infuriating to see two of my heroes denigrated by someone so obviously inferior to them. And then, quite by chance, about a month after the McCain remark, I happened to be reading a portion of Richard Wilbur's 1965 translation of the Molière play *Tartuffe* (1664). One passage captured my attention, and I urge you to read it thoroughly (it is written in verse, so it will also help if you read it aloud, and with an appropriate cadence):

> Those who have greatest cause for guilt and shame
> Are quickest to besmirch a neighbor's name.
> When there's a chance for libel, they never miss it;
> When something can be made to seem illicit
> They're off at once to spread the joyous news,
> Adding to fact what fantasies they choose.
> By talking up their neighbor's indiscretions
> They seek to camouflage their own transgressions,
> Hoping that others' innocent affairs
> Will lend a hue of innocence to theirs,
> Or that their own black guilt will come to seem
> Part of a general shady color-scheme.

Reading the passage, my immediate thought was, "Wow! That sounds a lot like Donald Trump." And, just to make sure Wilbur was accurately reflecting Molière's original intentions, I checked out a much earlier *Tartuffe* translation (by Curtis Hidden Page in 1908). The first two lines of the passage above were rendered in a slightly different way, but the message was the same:

> Those whose own conduct's most ridiculous,
> Are always quickest to speak ill of others.

It's difficult to fully recall my reaction when I first read these lines, but there was something deeply satisfying about seeing a contemporary figure described so accurately by someone writing three-and-a-half centuries earlier. I was so affected by the discovery that I made a mental note to be on the lookout for more quotations that brought Donald Trump to mind, and especially for ones that revealed something important about him.

As the weeks passed, I came across nearly a dozen additional quotations that captured something essentially true about this most unusual presidential candidate. These new discoveries made a deep impression on me, and I recall thinking, "Hmmm, I might be on to something here." I immediately created a *Trump File* on my computer. Some of the quotations in that new file—even though written centuries ago— could have been written about Trump's remarks about McCain's POW experiences or his role as head cheerleader of the "birther" movement:

> **There is nothing that more betrays a base, ungenerous spirit**
> **than the giving of secret stabs to a man's reputation.**
> JOSEPH ADDISON, in *The Spectator* (Mar. 27, 1711)

> **No sadder proof can be given**
> **by a man of his own littleness**
> **than disbelief in great men.**
> THOMAS CARLYLE, in *On Heroes, Hero-Worship,*
> *and the Heroic in History* (1841)

Almost immediately after Trump's remarks about McCain in that 2015 Iowa presidential forum, he was strongly denounced by fellow Republican presidential candidates Jeb Bush, Chris Christie, Lindsey Graham, Bobby Jindal, Rick Perry, Marco Rubio, and Scott Walker (some even called for Trump to withdraw from the race). But not all Republicans joined in, apparently choosing discretion over valor out of fear of alienating the Party's right-wing base. Rick Santorum and Ted Cruz praised McCain without denouncing Trump. And Ben Carson, while declining comment on Trump's shameful words, could only manage a feeble, ineffectual reply: "It depends on your definition of a war hero."

Since that first Molière quotation, I'd been searching for Trump-related observations, but some of my best new "finds" seemed more appropriate for those who were unwilling to challenge or criticize him (as with Santorum, Cruz, and Carson after the Iowa forum):

> **He who does not bellow the truth when he knows the truth**
> **makes himself the accomplice of liars and forgers.**
> CHARLES PÉGUY, in "Lettre du Provincial" (Dec. 21, 1899)

> **To sin by silence when we should protest,**
> **Makes cowards out of men.**
> ELLA WHEELER WILCOX, "Protest," in *Poems of Problems* (1914)

While I greatly treasured my newly discovered quotations, I wasn't planning to do anything with them because I was fairly certain that Donald Trump would be a short-lived political phenomenon. That feeling was strongly reinforced when *The National Review* came out with a special "Against Trump" issue in January of 2016. In that issue, which described Trump as "a menace to American conservatism," twenty-two prominent Republicans (including Glenn Beck, Mona Charen, Erick Erickson, William Kristol, and Thomas Sowell) all voiced their strong opposition to Trump, with most describing him as an ill-informed populist and not a true conservative.

I was thrilled to see this division among the Republicans, and soon began rooting for Trump to win his Party's nomination. My thought process was pretty straightforward. Since Hillary Clinton, the likely Democratic nominee was such a polarizing figure, I believed she would be in danger of losing a general election to a more palatable Republican candidate. A controversial and deeply flawed opponent like Trump was far preferable, and I made my feelings known to friends. Little did I know then that one day I'd be adding an unanticipated quotation to my *Trump File*:

> **We would often be sorry if our wishes were gratified.**
> AESOP, "The Old Man and Death," in *Fables* (6th c. BC)

But I'm getting ahead of myself. Trump went on to vanquish his primary opponents and, in July 2016, accepted the GOP's nomination for president. When Democrats nominated Hillary Clinton a week later, the two candidates were neck-and-neck in the national polls.

It was a brutal campaign with many twists and turns, including the FBI investigation of Clinton's e-mails, the chants of "Lock her up!" at Trump campaign rallies, Clinton's foolish "basket of deplorables" remark, Trump's bizarre "Russia, if you're listening" overture, the airing of the 2005 *Access Hollywood* tape, and the WikiLeaks e-mail dumps. Through it all, Clinton steadily increased her lead in the polls and, by the conclusion of the third presidential debate, most experts were predicting a landslide win. Three weeks before the election, Clinton was polling so far ahead of Trump that respected statistician Nate Silver set her chances of winning at 87.3 percent.

Less than two weeks before the election, things took a dramatic turn when FBI director James Comey informed Congress that he was re-opening the investigation into Clinton's e-mails (he had formally cleared her earlier in the campaign). Almost immediately, Clinton's lead in the polls began slipping. On November 6, 2016, two days before the election, Comey once again cleared Clinton of any wrongdoing. While the campaign had taken a serious hit, Clinton was still leading by a comfortable margin. On Election Day, Silver adjusted her chances of winning to 71.4 percent.

Joyce Carol Oates once wrote that "The blow you can't see coming is the blow that knocks you out," and Trump's highly unexpected victory on November 8, 2016 truly staggered me. It was the biggest upset in American political history, making the 1949 "Dewey Defeats Truman" newspaper headline seem like a quaint historical footnote. While Clinton won the popular vote by 2.8 million votes, Trump's razor-thin victories in a few key states gave him the electoral margin he needed.

I wish I could find a more eloquent way to state it, but I was in a state of shock. While I had never been a big Hillary Clinton fan, I happily—even enthusiastically—voted for her. In truth, though, mine was less a vote for Clinton than it was a vote against a man I had long regarded as a textbook narcissist.

The day after the election, I was faced with an almost nightmarish reality: the country I loved was soon to be led by a superficial and self-absorbed blowhard. I was especially worried about an American president whose deep-seated insecurity—constantly in need of being propped up by his own puffery and bombast—would make him highly susceptible to flattery and manipulation. I also greatly feared that revered American institutions would be eroded by a person with a long-standing history of lying and deception, a disturbing pattern of admiration for autocratic strong men, and a dangerously limited grasp of world history. To paraphrase the philosopher and essayist George Santayana, it's hard to avoid repeating the mistakes of the past when you haven't read a history book in fifty years, if ever.

Yes, you could say I was having trouble coping with the new reality. I had difficulty concentrating. My mind constantly went back to some unsettling aspect of the campaign. Or it moved warily into the future as I began to imagine some predictable "elections have consequences" scenario. For the first time in decades, I had trouble getting to sleep at night. And then, after finally dozing off, I often slept fitfully. I was also angry—*very* angry—at the thought of ninety million eligible voters deciding to sit out the election.

In my everyday interactions with people, I noticed that I was smiling and laughing less, and I believe I was even drinking a little more than usual. As a psychologist, I was showing all the signs of what people in my profession call a *reactive depression*. The specific nature of the depression was not to be found in any of the official diagnostic manuals, so I gave it my own name: Trump Adjustment Disorder.

I had experienced a few bouts of depression earlier in my life, so I decided to do something I'd found helpful in the past: reading. Not just any reading, but strategic and targeted reading. Reading with a purpose, you might say.

Reading for therapeutic or mental health purposes has long been called *bibliotherapy*, which the *American Heritage Dictionary* defines this way: "A form of supportive psychotherapy in which carefully selected reading materials are used to assist a subject in solving personal problems." The practice occupies an honored place in history:

> To acquire the habit of reading is to construct for yourself
> a refuge from almost all the miseries of life.
> W. SOMERSET MAUGHAM, in *Books and You* (1940)

> Study has been my sovereign remedy
> against the worries of life.
> I have never had a care that an hour's
> reading could not dispel.
> CHARLES DE MONTESQUIEU, in *My Thoughts, 1720-55*

Reading had pretty much saved my life when I read *Walden* during my junior year in college. And I've had numerous Jewish and Christian friends who've sworn that the practice of daily Scripture reading has performed the same function for them. In contrast to heart-to-heart conversations with a close friend or consultations with a counselor or therapist, a systematic and focused reading regimen allows us to spend multiple hours every week with some of history's greatest minds and finest thinkers. In his *Discourse on Method* (1637), René Descartes expressed it well:

> To read good books is like holding a conversation
> with the most eminent minds of past centuries
> and, moreover, a studied conversation
> in which these authors reveal to us
> only the best of their thoughts.

Happily, I had already made some progress on the bibliotherapy front with the *Trump File* I started back in 2015. And while that compilation contained several dozen wonderful quotations, it was clear that I was in need of a larger therapeutic dosage to combat my current situation.

Shortly after beginning my new reading regimen, a number of friends forwarded me a 1920 observation from H. L. Mencken that was making the rounds. The quotation appeared to be just what I was looking for, but there was something a little "too good to be true" about it. Sure enough, as with so many quotations passed around on the internet, it was based on a real quotation, but riddled with errors. I was soon able to discover the original—and accurate—version, and it was spectacular:

> **As democracy is perfected, the office [of US president]**
> **represents more and more closely,**
> **the inner soul of the people.**
> **On some great and glorious day, the plain folks**
> **of the land will reach their heart's desire at last, and**
> **the White House will be adorned by a downright moron.**
>
> H. L. MENCKEN, "Bayard v. Lionheart," in *The Baltimore Evening Sun* (July 26, 1920)

The word *prescient* is often used for quotations from the past that illuminate a present moment—and Mencken's sardonic observation clearly fits that description. Almost immediately, I began a systematic search for similar nuggets from my favorite writers. As in all prospecting, it took some serious digging, but, to tweak an old saying, there's gold in them there books. Two examples from world literature will make the point.

In Dostoevsky's *The Brothers Karamazov* (1880), the patriarch of the family, Fyodor Pavlovich Karamazov, is a character who bears a remarkable similarity to Donald Trump—he is vain, insecure, buffoonish, and prone to gratuitous lying. Early in the novel, after he meets a spiritual adviser named Father Zosima, he asks the religious leader for his opinion about what he needs to do to inherit eternal life.

Father Zosima immediately replies that people should not lie, especially to themselves. He continues: "A man who lies to himself and listens to his own lie comes *to a point where he does not discern any truth either in himself or anywhere around him* [italics mine], and thus falls into disrespect towards himself and others." After continuing with a few more thoughts on the problem of lying to oneself, Father Zosima concludes:

> **A man who lies to himself is often the first to take offense.**
> **It sometimes feels very good to take offense, doesn't it?**
> **And surely he knows that no one has offended him,**
> **and that he himself has invented the offense**
> **and told lies just for the beauty of it,**
> **that he has exaggerated for the sake of effect, that he has**
> **picked on a word and made a mountain out of a pea—**
> **he knows all of that, and still he is the first to take offense,**
> **he likes feeling offended, it gives him great pleasure,**
> **and thus he reaches the point of real hostility.**

As an experiment, I showed this passage—without any other information—to twenty people (equally divided between liberals and conservatives), and asked the question: "Who is being described here?" *Every single person* answered "Donald Trump."

To be perfectly honest, though, the two groups tended to answer the question in a slightly different manner. While the liberals almost delighted in citing Trump, the conservatives tended to be more circumspect, or even suspicious, saying things like, "I would imagine the author is describing Trump here." But the fact that *all of them* identified Trump was a pretty remarkable result, given that the passage came from a book written 135 years before Trump began spewing out his daily tweets. Carl Jung was clearly thinking about something along these same lines when he wrote in his 1960 book *Synchronicity*:

**It is sometimes difficult to avoid the impression
that there is a sort of foreknowledge
of the coming series of events.**

The nugget I found in the *Karamazov* novel gave me the equivalent of "gold fever," and I was soon panning for more treasures in the great stream of world literature. In less than a week, I had another strike. This one came from *Hadji Murad,* one of Leo Tolstoy's lesser-known novels, written late in his life and published posthumously in 1912. The book is a fictionalized account of a mid-nineteenth century Chechen rebel who was fighting against the forced incorporation of his country into Tsar Nicholas I's Russian Empire.

Tolstoy took a dim view of Nicholas I, and his book offers a number of passages that depict him as vain, ineffectual, and highly susceptible to flattery. At one point, after Nicholas was praised by one his aides, the narrator says of him: "This praise of his strategic abilities was especially pleasing to Nicholas, because, *though he was proud of his strategic abilities, at the bottom of his heart he was aware that he had none* [italics mine]. And now he wanted to hear more detailed praise of himself."

A bit later in the novel, the narrator offered an assessment of the Russian ruler that spoke directly to one of the greatest fears many have had about a Trump presidency:

**The constant, obvious flattery, contrary to all evidence,
of the people around him had brought him to the point
that he no longer saw his contradictions,
no longer conformed his actions and words to reality, logic,
or even simple common sense, but was fully convinced that
all his orders, however senseless, unjust, and inconsistent
with each other, became sensible, just, and
consistent with each other only because he gave them.**

It is no exaggeration to say that I found the Dostoevsky and Tolstoy passages almost mesmerizing. I found myself going back to them again and again. If I'd been harboring any doubts about my own personal assessment of our new president, these authors were providing a form of corroboration, essentially saying: "No, you're not crazy; people like Trump have been around for centuries."

These powerful literary passages also reminded me of something I'd long known intellectually, but was now experiencing personally—that works of fiction put psychology textbooks to shame when it comes to providing a true glimpse into the nature of human beings. Even more important, they planted ideas in my mind that might never have occurred to me by simply thinking on my own or commiserating with friends. The German writer Arthur Schopenhauer was clearly thinking about something similar to my recent experiences when he wrote in *Parerga and Paralipomena* (1851):

> **Reading is equivalent to thinking with
> someone else's head instead of with one's own.**

If observations from the past can have a prescient quality—as we saw with that Mencken quotation earlier—they can also have a compelling, even startling, one. You'll see hundreds of examples later on, but three quickly come to mind. The first was offered in a 1760 letter Samuel Adams wrote to his friend James Warren:

> **If ever the time should come when vain & aspiring men
> shall possess the highest seats in government,
> our country will stand in need
> of its experienced patriots to prevent its ruin.**

The second appeared in a 1936 speech in Albany, New York, by Albert Einstein:

Desire for approval and recognition is a healthy motive;
but the desire to be acknowledged as better, stronger,
or more intelligent...easily leads to an excessively
egoistic psychological adjustment which may become
injurious for the individual and for the community.

And the third appeared in *The Grand Chessboard*, a 1997 book from Zbigniew Brzezinski, the National Security Adviser during the Jimmy Carter administration:

We have a large public that is
very ignorant about public affairs
and very susceptible to simplistic slogans
by candidates who appear out of nowhere,
have no track record, but mouth appealing slogans.

As I continued my reading and research efforts during the first year of the Trump presidency, it became clear that a rule of thumb had been guiding my efforts. If a quotation made me think, "That brings Donald Trump to mind," I added it to my files. One could even say that this became my *reigning idea,* a concept I borrowed from the Irish writer Maria Edgeworth, who had written in her 1817 novel *Harrington*:

When the mind is full of any one subject,
that subject seems to recur with extraordinary frequency—
it appears to pursue or to meet us at every turn;
in every conversation that we hear—in every book
we open—in every newspaper we take up,
the reigning idea recurs, and then we are surprised,
and exclaim at these wonderful coincidences.

As the months progressed, my life was filled with a multitude of wonderful coincidences that resulted in scores of new quotations being added to my expanding collection of quotations, including:

**Vanity working on a weak head
produces every sort of mischief.**
JANE AUSTEN, in *Emma* (1815)

**Life is so very simple when you have
no facts to confuse you.**
PEG BRACKEN, in *A Window Over the Sink* (1981)

Only the very ignorant are perfectly satisfied that they know.
ROBERT G. INGERSOLL, in *Liberty in Literature* (1890)

Guard against the impostures of pretended patriotism.
GEORGE WASHINGTON, in his Farewell Address (Sep. 17, 1796)

As wonderful as it was to discover these new, fresh, and previously unknown quotations, it was equally satisfying to begin to see familiar quotations in a new way—especially those that didn't initially look like candidates for my collection:

A little learning is a dangerous thing.
ALEXANDER POPE, in *An Essay on Criticism* (1711)

This is one of history's most famous sayings—and also one of the most misunderstood.

In offering the thought, Pope was suggesting that a small amount of knowledge ("a little learning") is not typically going to put people in danger, but it can become dangerous in circumstances when thorough or extensive knowledge is required. The problem he was attempting to describe shows up most commonly when shallow and superficial people make the mistake of believing they know more than they do. When people with *a little learning* are confronted with a problem whose solution demands real knowledge, they become dangerous to themselves, and to others. This problem has been well-expressed in modern times as well, as when Larry McMurtry wrote in *Lonesome Dove* (1985):

Incompetents invariably make trouble
for people other than themselves.

Except for a tiny group of quotation confidants, I didn't discuss my bibliotherapy project with anybody—not even my wife Katherine— but one day, a person familiar with my work asked if I'd been working on anything new. When I gave her a brief description, she brightened with interest and asked if my file contained any quotations from the Bible. I was delighted to report that I'd found about a dozen relevant biblical passages, including a new one (new to me, at least) that I had discovered a few days earlier:

Let another man praise thee, and not thine own mouth.
BOOK OF PROVERBS 27:2

She was familiar with the passage, and added that there were similar biblical injunctions about boasting that might deserve inclusion in the book. As our conversation ended, she added, "I'm sure your collection also includes Jesus's famous words about the exalted being humbled." I confessed that it did not, and promised to add it soon. That promise resulted in a foray into Scripture that went on for more than a month. In an exercise that proved both exhilarating and eye-opening, I ultimately came upon nearly a hundred passages that seemed relevant in any discussion of the Bible and Donald Trump. Here's a typical example:

Where there is no vision, the people perish.
BOOK OF PROVERBS 29:18

There are few people—even among Trump's most fervent support-ers—who would describe him as a man of vision. Given the biblical warning about people perishing when their leaders have no vision, one would expect conservative Christians to be greatly troubled by this particular failing. And while it's true that a few—a *very* few—have acknowledged Trump's lack of vision, the great majority of his base have simply decided to ignore the deficit.

How could a man with a lack of vision win the enthusiastic support of so many people who describe themselves as devout Christians? The answer lies in a fascinating mental trick called *rationalization*. As the name suggests, rationalization occurs when people attempt to find an acceptable *rationale* for things that, deep down, they know are not acceptable. In *Philosophy: Who Needs It* (1982), Ayn Rand described it this way:

Rationalization is a cover-up,
a process of providing one's emotions with a false identity,
of giving them spurious explanations and justifications—
in order to hide one's motives,
not just from others, but primarily from oneself.

Rationalizing is not about perceiving reality, said Rand, but "of attempting to make reality fit one's emotions." When we take what is real and adjust it to our emotions, we're not only *distorting* reality, we're fooling ourselves. For this reason, psychoanalyst Karen Horney aptly described rationalization as "self-deception by reasoning."

To any reasonably objective observer, Trump's support from the religious right stemmed directly from his campaign promise to appoint Supreme Court justices who would help overturn *Roe v. Wade*. Instead of frankly acknowledging Trump's support for their anti-abortion efforts, however, American evangelicals were more frequently seen praising a politician who was willing to speak his mind. Or robotically repeating the refrain about draining the swamp. Or enthusing about how wonderful it would be to have a great businessman in the White House (a position that conveniently ignored what almost all serious analysts believed about Trump's business acumen). These obvious rationalizations all brought to mind a saying long attributed to the American financier J. P. Morgan:

**A man always has two reasons for what he does—
a good one, and the real one.**

Conservative Christians also had to ignore a mountain of evidence regarding Trump's history of amorality and immorality (including multiple adulterous affairs while married, an unconscionable pattern of failing to pay people who worked for him, and his infamous *Access Hollywood* admission about sexual assaults on women). When attempting to explain the willful ignorance of Trump supporters, many political observers began to cite the familiar English proverb: "There are none so blind as those who will not see." While this *is* a wonderful saying—and *did* accurately describe the situation—its continued repetition was getting a bit tiresome. I was delighted when one day I came across a little-known quotation that even better described the phenomenon:

**There are conditions of blindness so voluntary
that they become complicity.**
PAUL BOURGET, in *Cosmopolis* (1892)

When I first began my bibliotherapy efforts, my *Trump File* contained only a handful of quotations. A few short years later, my thinking had been stimulated by what seemed like an unending series of observations from great thinkers and writers. As a result, I had arrived at a far better understanding of what had happened—and why—in the 2016 presidential election. I also had a better grasp of the new political realities confronting our nation. But most important of all, the confusion, distraction, depression, and other mental health issues that originally inspired my reading regimen were gone. You could say that I was back to my normal self, but I believe it's more accurate to say that I had become an improved version of my normal self.

Within weeks of the inauguration of the new president, I found myself doing things I'd never done before, or hadn't done in decades. I began writing letters to the editors of local newspapers. I made regular phone calls to the offices of our two US senators to express my opinion on upcoming legislation and other matters. I participated in a number of political rallies and protest demonstrations. I volunteered to work on a congressional campaign, something I hadn't done since Gene McCarthy's 1972 run for the presidency. I made financial contributions to a whole bunch of political campaigns around the country—and was thrilled when my dollars helped in some small way to elect about a dozen congressional candidates in the 2018 mid-term elections.

I even summoned up the wherewithal to challenge the thinking of a number of people who either voted for Trump or didn't vote at all in the 2016 election. Not all of those conversations went as well as I'd hoped, but I did make some progress with a few of the less fanatical Trump supporters, and even secured a number of personal commitments from some of the apathetic ones to vote in the next election.

As I reflected on the changes that had occurred in me over the past three years, it became clear that the election of Donald Trump—so very problematical at the beginning—helped me become a more active and engaged citizen. And, as with so many other things I've experienced in life, my personal evolution was captured in some wonderful quotations:

> **There is no such thing as a problem**
> **without a gift for you in its hands.**
>
> RICHARD BACH, in *Illusions: The Adventures*
> *of a Reluctant Messiah* (1977)

> **Truth, however bitter, can be accepted,**
> **and woven into a design for living.**
>
> AGATHA CHRISTIE, Hercule Poirot speaking, in *The Hollow* (1946)

From Personal File to Quotation Anthology

As 2018 drew to a close, I was ready to resume my regular writing routine and begin work on a new book. Over the past twenty years,

I'd come out with seven books in the "word and language" genre. My books were the natural consequence of a quotation collecting habit I began when I was a college junior. The very first was *Never Let a Fool Kiss You or a Kiss Fool You*, a 1999 book that attempted to bring the obscure literary device of *chiasmus* (ky-AZ-muss) out of the closet and into the world of popular usage, and that book was followed by six more.[1] Like many authors, I was considering several possible projects, but hadn't yet selected *the next one*.

I often launch major new projects at the beginning of a new year, so on the first day of 2019, I sat down to make a decision. I narrowed it down to two possibilities, but at the end of the day, was unable to commit to one or the other. In his 1954 novel *Sweet Thursday*, John Steinbeck wrote that matters are often clarified or resolved "after the committee of sleep has worked on it," so I decided to postpone the decision until the next day. The next morning, I woke up with a new and clear thought in my mind:

Why not turn your personal project into a book?

That was the precise moment I decided to turn my *Trump File* into the *Deconstructing Trump* book you are reading right now. That it took so long for such an obvious idea to surface still mystifies me, for in hindsight it seems like such a no-brainer. I had benefited greatly from my bibliotherapy efforts over the past few years, so it made sense to make the complete collection available to others as well, particularly those who've struggled with the reality of a Trump presidency.

After I bring this Introduction to a close, I will present to you *The Deconstructing Trump Quotation Anthology*, my attempt to provide a unique historical perspective on what historians will ultimately call The Trump Phenomenon. The compilation will consist of 1,000 quotations, most standing alone, but some with an explanatory note or a bit

---

1 *Oxymoronica* (2004), *Viva la Repartee* (2005), *I Never Metaphor I Didn't Like* (2008), *Ifferisms* (2009), *Neverisms* (2011), and *Metaphors Be With You* (2016).

of commentary from me. At the beginning of the *Anthology*, I'll offer a few additional thoughts about its nature and contents.

The primary audience for this book is people who—like me—have experienced a case of what I've been calling Trump Adjustment Disorder. As I mentioned earlier, it's not a condition you will find formally described in the professional literature, but people with the condition generally know when they have it. If you're such a person—or you know such a person—this book might be part of an effective treatment plan.

If your first thought is "The most effective treatment is to resoundingly defeat Trump in the next presidential election," I heartily agree. But that next election will not come for many more months. In the meantime, I hope this book will provide some temporary relief before the final curtain is drawn on the Trump presidency on November 3, 2020.

A Brief Note About the Title

Over the past half century, I've seen countless newspaper, magazine, and journal articles that claimed to be *deconstructing* a specific individual (Shakespeare, Freud, Marx) or a large topic like slavery, feminism, and the post-Civil War Reconstruction era (and, yes, that one was cleverly titled "Deconstructing Reconstruction"). In the past fifteen years, I've also seen scores of articles, editorials, blog posts, and op-ed pieces that *deconstructed* a particular policy of the Bush, Obama, or Trump presidencies. (I even recall a 2005 article from *The Boston Globe* titled "Deconstructing Cheney.")

I've always been drawn to the term *deconstruction*, but had only a vague idea of what it actually meant. After a number of attempts to educate myself, I confess that I was not particularly successful (it *is* a challenging subject). I'm glad I did the research, though, for I discovered that the meaning of the term has been slowly evolving as it moved from academia to popular parlance.

A few years back, the *Encyclopedia Britannica* editors noted this trend when they wrote: "In popular usage, the term has come to mean a critical dismantling of tradition and traditional modes of thought." It seems clear to me that the term has continued to evolve, and now means something closer to "a critical dismantling" of anything—or any person—being skeptically scrutinized. The underlying idea goes something like this: If an accepted reality or popular narrative has been falsely or misleadingly *constructed*, it can be *deconstructed*.

Most dictionaries have not yet caught up with the evolving meaning of the term, and I was pleased to discover that the folks at *Merriam-Webster* were keeping current. Their online dictionary contains two definitions of *deconstruction*, including this one:

> **The analytic examination of something...**
> **often in order to reveal its inadequacy.**

Reading it, I thought, "That works for me!" and *Deconstructing Trump* was born.

A Message for Voters

There will almost certainly be one more presidential election with Trump's name at the head of the ticket—and this one just might be worthy of the over-used designation, "The most consequential election of our lifetime." If you're a regular voter, you probably understand what I'm talking about. And as a regular voter, you're exactly the kind of person Winston Churchill honored in a memorable 1944 House of Commons speech (note my one small addition to his remarks in brackets):

> At the bottom of all the tributes paid to democracy
> is the little man [and woman], walking into
> the little booth, with a little pencil, making
> a little cross on a little bit of paper—
> no amount of rhetoric or voluminous
> discussion can possibly diminish
> the overwhelming importance of that point.

Given your history, you'll likely be voting again in 2020—and whether Trump or the Democratic Party's nominee is your choice, I salute your involvement in the process.

Not everyone in your world will be joining you at the polls, though, including many of your neighbors, coworkers, and casual acquaintances. When these folks don't vote, you may disapprove, but you don't find it particularly upsetting. It's another matter entirely, however, when the person choosing not to vote is a mate, a child, a close friend, a dear cousin, or a favorite niece or nephew. After the last election, the theme of *people-I-care-about-not-caring-to-vote* emerged all over the nation—and it resulted in millions of frustrating and unproductive conversations.

If this matter continues to stick in your craw, I have a suggestion. After you finish reading this book, lend it to a special someone who didn't vote in the 2016 election (if you want to keep your copy, consider purchasing it as a gift or holiday present). Don't even broach the subject of voting; just say you thought they would enjoy the book.

A Message for 2016 Non-Voters

As I was bringing this book to completion, I was fond of saying to friends that I would be thrilled beyond comprehension if it were helpful in getting only one non-voter in the last election to cast a ballot in the next one. Perhaps that single non-voter will be you.

If you didn't vote in the last election, you're a member of the largest and most important segment of the American electorate—the 90 to 95 million people who were *eligible to vote* in the election *but did not.* Your numbers dwarf the 65.8 million who voted for Clinton, and the 63 million who voted for Trump.

It's possible you received this book as a gift or as a loaner from a friend or family member who dearly wishes you would give some thought to changing your pattern and getting back to the polls. I'm not going to pile on with another lecture (you've probably heard enough of those already). I'm simply going to ask one question: "Are you happy with Donald Trump as the president of the United States?"

If your answer is yes, I don't care what you do in 2020. But if your answer is no, let me remind you of something Plato wrote in *The Republic* (4th c. BC):

> **One of the penalties for refusing to participate in politics is that you end up being governed by your inferiors.**

A Final Word

One never knows for sure when the "deciding moment" in one's life is going to come, but we know from the study of history that many have been precipitated by an encounter with a single book. In *Walden* (1854), Henry David Thoreau wrote:

> **How many a man has dated a new era in his life from the reading of a book.**

For Thoreau, the book was Emerson's *Nature* (1836). For me—and countless others—the book was *Walden*. Thoreau introduced the thought above by writing: "There are probably words addressed to our condition exactly, which, if we could really hear and understand, would be more salutary than the morning or spring to our lives, and possibly put a new aspect on the face of things for us."

I hope *Deconstructing Trump* will be the book that will date a new era in your life. It is certainly not a classic (few quotation anthologies in history have achieved that status), but it does contain a multitude of classic thoughts that may help you put a new aspect on the face of things. If it does, drop me a note at: drmgrothe@aol.com.

If you sat out the 2016 contest but decide to vote in the 2020 election, let me know that as well—and why. If I hear from enough people, I'll likely write an article titled "Why Non-Voters in 2016 Voted in 2020." And if you like, I'll even send you a draft before I submit it for publication.

In his 1844 poem "The Present Crisis," the American poet James Russell Lowell was writing about the problem of slavery, and his words have relevance to a crisis of a different nature in our current era:

> **Once to every man and nation comes**
> **The moment to decide,**
> **In the strife of Truth with Falsehood,**
> **For the good or evil side.**

The Deconstructing Trump Quotation Anthology

Donald Trump and
the Trump Phenomenon
Through the Lens of
Quotation History

The Deconstructing Trump Quotation Anthology consists of 1,000 quotations that attempt to shed a revealing light on Donald J. Trump and The Trump Era.

Donald Trump is not, however, featured in any one of the 1,000 quotations. None mention his name. Not one was even written in this century. And yet, a great many—even though written decades or centuries ago—capture the essence of Trump and Trumpism so precisely that one might easily believe they were written in the past year or so.

In this brief prologue to the anthology, I simply want to: (1) give you a better idea about what's coming; (2) discuss the principal value of a good quotation anthology; and (3) offer a few recommendations about how to best approach this book.

What You Will Find in This Anthology

This is an A-to-Z quotation anthology, meaning it is organized alphabetically by the last name of the author (there are 25 sections, one for every letter of the alphabet, except "X"). The overwhelming majority of the quotations look very much like the book's very first and very last entries. I'm reproducing them below:

> **An empty man is full of himself.**
> EDWARD ABBEY, in *A Voice Crying in the Wilderness* (1990)

> **If you shut up truth and bury it under the ground,**
> **it will but grow, and gather to itself**
> **such explosive power**
> **that the day it bursts through**
> **it will blow up everything in its way.**
> ÉMILE ZOLA, in an open letter in the French
> newspaper *L'Aurore* (Jan. 13, 1898)

All entries have the same format: the featured quotation in bold type, followed by the author's name and the original source. After you read each of the entries, I urge you to pause for just a moment to consider what the precise Trump "connection" might be.

When I took a moment to reflect on the "An empty man is full of himself" quotation, for example, I had an "aha!" moment. I'd seen Abbey's characterization of self-absorbed people a number of times over the past couple of decades, but *never before* had I associated it with a specific human being. Now I can't see the quotation without thinking of Trump. This same thing has happened with hundreds of quotations I've discovered in the past couple of years.

With the Zola quotation, my mind immediately went to the many truths Trump has buried about his tax returns, his precise involvement with Russian operatives and oligarchs, and the myriad other secrets in his life. When the ugly truth about these matters finally bursts through—as it ultimately will—the result will almost certainly be explosive.

The quotations from Abbey and Zola are stand-alone entries, and are illustrative of the vast majority of the quotations in the anthology. Occasionally, though, I've decided to add a brief note or personal commentary. Here are two examples:

> **The man who knows nothing thinks he is**
> **teaching others what he has just learned himself.**
> JEAN DE LA BRUYÈRE, in *The Characters* (1688)
>
> When Trump says, "Nobody knows," "People don't realize," "A lot of people don't know," or similar expressions, it has become an inside joke among journalists that they all mean the same thing: "I had no clue about this until somebody filled me in recently." Eli Stokel, a *Washington Post* journalist, described the frequent use of such phrases as "Trump's tells." When he says such things, Stokel suggests, it should be interpreted as: "That's code for I just found this out."

What a sweep of vanity comes this way.
WILLIAM SHAKESPEARE, in *Timon of Athens* (c. 1607)

This is a minor character's remark at the sight of an approaching group of women, all dressed in Amazon costumes, dancing, and playing lutes. The *sweep of vanity* saying has not yet been used by any of Trump's critics or political opponents, but it's such a delicious phrase that I expect it will soon be showing up on the campaign trail.

I do these periodic *quotation-plus-notation* entries for two reasons. First, I've learned so much while doing my research that I wanted to share some of that knowledge with you. The second goes to the very heart of all quotation anthologies. No matter how interesting the topic, a pattern of quotation after quotation after quotation can become repetitive, and even tiresome. I have over 400 quotation anthologies in my personal library, and my favorites are the ones in which the compilers have occasionally offered brief explanatory notes, quotation backstories, or personal observations. I hope you will appreciate my doing the same for you.

The Principle Value of a Quotation Anthology

In her autobiography *Time to Be in Earnest* (1999), the English writer P. D. James wrote:

**Books of quotations...afford me one of the most
undemanding but satisfying forms of reading pleasure.**

After that lovely word *satisfying*, the key word here is *undemanding*. If you want to learn more about the writings of, say, G. K. Chesterton, or Henry David Thoreau, or Albert Einstein, you could spend months or years reading their various books and essays.

Or you could read Kevin Belmont's *The Quotable Chesterton* (2011). Or Jeffrey S. Cramer's *The Portable Thoreau* (1964). Or Alice Calaprice's *The New Quotable Einstein* (2005).

You could read any one of these books in a week or two. I wouldn't recommend it, for quotation anthologies are not meant for reading in a traditional sense—they're meant for browsing, sampling, and dipping into when you want to take a plunge. But you *could* read a quotation anthology in a week or so. That is, you could read in a relatively short period of time a book that took the compiler many thousands of hours to prepare. When you pick up a quotation anthology, you become the beneficiary of someone else's labor of love. As P. D. James suggested in her observation above, it's both satisfying *and* undemanding.

So, let's say you're interested in a question that might be posed this way: "If they were living today, what would history's greatest writers, thinkers, and political leaders have to say about Donald Trump's ascendancy to the US presidency? And what might they add about the social, cultural, and political factors that led to his unexpected victory?"

If this is something you'd like to learn more about, then I'm your man (or, if you like, your *designated researcher*). Over the past four years, I've engaged in something close to 5,000 hours of research to compile and comment on a thousand quotations that you can peruse in a fraction of the time.

How to Approach This Book

Let me bring this prologue to a close by offering a few suggestions about how to best approach this book. First, and most important, an anthology is not a typical book, so don't even think about starting from the beginning and reading it straight through. Remember, an anthology is meant to be browsed and sampled.

Don't read too quickly. Don't read too much at any one sitting. And pause occasionally to reflect on the meaning or significance of an observation. The best quotation anthologies are extremely stimulating, so let your thinking be provoked. Set the book in your lap every now and then, close your eyes, and think about what you've just read. If an idea pops into your mind, jot it down before it slips away. Periodically throughout the book, I've provided blank pages that may come in handy.

When you come across a "Wow!" quotation, share it with someone. Not all of the quotations in this anthology will bowl you over, but some will, I promise you (and, quite likely, more than you are expecting). When this happens, set the book aside and share the quotation with a person you believe will appreciate it as much as you do.

The final thing I'd like you to do is for my benefit, not yours. If you spot any typographical errors or other mistakes, please let me know. And if you know—or happen to come across—any quotations that I might have missed or overlooked, please pass 'em along. I can be reached at: drmgrothe@aol.com.

I also have a website where you can delve further into the topic, learn more about me and my other books, catch some of my media appearances, or sign up for my free weekly e-newsletter ("Dr. Mardy's Quotes of the Week"). Come up and visit sometime: www.deconstructingtrump.com.

**When people show
you who they are,
believe them.**

Maya Angelou

An empty man is full of himself.

EDWARD ABBEY, in *A Voice Crying in the Wilderness* (1990)

The great corrupter of public men is the ego....
Looking in the mirror
distracts one's attention from the problem.

DEAN ACHESON, in speech to Society of
American Historians (Mar. 31, 1966)

How is it possible,
that the love of gain and the lust of domination
should render the human mind so callous to
every principle of honor, generosity, and benevolence?

ABIGAIL ADAMS, in letter to husband John Adams (July 25, 1775)

Several decades later, Mrs. Adams grew deeply concerned over how
this "love of gain and lust of domination" began to infect political
parties. In an 1804 letter to president Thomas Jefferson, she warned:
"Party hatred, by its deadly poison, blinds the eyes and envenoms the
heart. It is fatal to the integrity of the moral character."

Many of our disappointments and much of our unhappiness
arise from our forming false notions of things and persons.

ABIGAIL ADAMS, in 1761 letter to Mrs. H. Lincoln

A common mistake that people make
when trying to design something completely foolproof
was to underestimate the ingenuity of complete fools.

DOUGLAS ADAMS, in *Mostly Harmless* (1992)

Elections are won by men and women
chiefly because most people vote against
somebody, rather than for somebody.

FRANKLIN P. ADAMS, in *Nods and Becks* (1944)

The trouble with this country is that
there are too many politicians
who believe, with a conviction based on experience,
that you can fool all of the people all of the time.

FRANKLIN P. ADAMS, in *Nods and Becks* (1944)

This observation tweaks a saying that every schoolchild will tell you comes from Abraham Lincoln: "You can fool all of the people some of the time; you can fool some of the people all of the time; but you can't fool all of the people all the time."

Lincoln scholars, however, are in agreement that the 16th US president never said anything like this (the saying first began to be attributed to him two decades after his death). According to quotation sleuth Garson O'Toole, the basic idea was originally expressed centuries earlier, when the French scholar Jacques Abbadie wrote in a 1684 treatise: "One can fool some men, or fool all men in some places and times, but one cannot fool all men in all places and ages."

Practical politics consists in ignoring facts.

HENRY BROOKS ADAMS, in *The Education of Henry Adams* (1907)

Politics, as a practice, whatever its professions,
has always been the systematic organization of hatreds.

HENRY BROOKS ADAMS, in *The Education of Henry Adams* (1907)

The effect of power and publicity on all men is the
aggravation of self, a sort of tumor
that ends by killing the victim's sympathies.
>   HENRY BROOKS ADAMS, in *The Education of Henry Adams* (1907)

I pray Heaven to bestow
the best of blessings on this House
and all that shall hereafter inhabit it.
May none but honest and wise men
ever rule under this roof.
>   JOHN ADAMS, in letter to Abigail Adams (Nov. 2, 1800),
>   upon moving into the newly constructed White House

It is a very great mistake to imagine that
the object of loyalty is the authority and
interest of one individual man.
>   SAMUEL ADAMS, "Loyalty and Sedition,"
>   in *The Public Advertiser* (Jan., 1748).

The "one individual man" in question here was, of course, the English monarch. Adams, who was only twenty-six when he wrote these words, believed that blind loyalty to George II had led millions into "dependence and submission."

After writing that "The true object of loyalty is a good legal constitution," Adams continued with a passage that rings as true today as when it was originally written: "Whoever, therefore, insinuates notions of government contrary to the constitution, or in any degree winks at any measures to suppress or even to weaken it, is not a loyal man."

If ever the time should come when vain & aspiring men
shall possess the highest seats in government,
our country will stand in need
of its experienced patriots to prevent its ruin.

SAMUEL ADAMS, in 1760 letter to James Warren

It is easy to become the dupe of a deferred purpose,
of the promise the future can never keep.

JANE ADDAMS, in *Twenty Years at Hull House* (1910)

Trump's campaign promise to build a border wall that would be paid for by Mexico fit perfectly into a "deferred purpose" category, and even though transparently ridiculous from the beginning, it duped millions with surprising ease.

There is nothing that more betrays a base, ungenerous spirit
than the giving of secret stabs to a man's reputation.

JOSEPH ADDISON, in *The Spectator* (Mar. 27, 1711)

A man must be excessively stupid, as well as uncharitable,
who believes there is no virtue but on his own side,
and that there are not men as honest as himself
who may differ from him in political principles.

JOSEPH ADDISON, in *The Spectator* (Dec. 8, 1711)

It is well known that those who
do not trust themselves never trust others.

ALFRED ADLER, in *Understanding Human Nature* (1928)

This maxim about self-trust has been well known for centuries. In his *Memoirs* (1717), the French clergyman known to history as Cardinal de Retz expressed it this way: "A man who does not trust himself will never really trust anybody."

> One of the frightening things about our
> time is the number of people who think
> it is a form of intellectual audacity to be stupid.
> A whole generation seems to be taking
> on an easy distrust of thought.
>
> RENATA ADLER, in *A Year in the Dark* (1969)

> Those who prosper take on airs of vanity.
>
> AESCHYLUS, in *Agamemnon* (5th c. BC)

> A prosperous fool is a grievous burden.
>
> AESCHYLUS, in *Fragments* (5th c. BC)

> Everyone's quick to blame the alien.
>
> AESCHYLUS, in *The Suppliant Maidens* (5th c. BC)

> Those who assume a character which
> does not belong to them,
> only make themselves ridiculous.
>
> AESOP, "The Crow and the Raven," in *Fables* (6th c. BC)

> A liar will not be believed,
> even when he speaks the truth.
>
> AESOP, "The Shepherd's Boy," in *Fables* (6th c. BC)

This is history's first saying about a problem that is now often described as a lack of credibility. A few centuries later, Aristotle offered a similar observation about people who are careless with the truth (see his entry below). In 2018, after President Trump claimed that Michael Wolff's *Fire and Fury* book was "a pack of lies," Wolff shot back: "My credibility is being questioned by a man who has less credibility than, perhaps, anyone who has ever walked on Earth."

> **Fine clothes may disguise,**
> **but foolish words will disclose a fool.**
> AESOP, "The Ass in the Lion's Skin," in *Fables* (6th c. BC)

> **We would often be sorry if our wishes were gratified.**
> AESOP, "The Old Man and Death," in *Fables* (6th c. BC)

> **The truth which makes men free is for the most part**
> **the truth which men prefer not to hear.**
> JOHN AGAR, tweaking John 8:32, in *A Time for Greatness* (1942)

> **To be ignorant of one's ignorance**
> **is the malady of the ignorant.**
> A. BRONSON ALCOTT, in *Table Talk* (1877)

> **Patriotism is a lively sense of collective responsibility.**
> **Nationalism is a silly cock crowing on its own dunghill.**
> RICHARD ALDINGTON, in *The Colonel's Daughter* (1931)

You'll find a number of nationalism versus patriotism quotations in this collection (see entries by Clarke, de Gaulle, Harris, and Orwell), but this one may be the best. On the specific subject of nationalism, Albert Einstein described it most accurately when he called it an infantile way of thinking (see the Einstein entry below).

Ridicule is man's most potent weapon.
It is almost impossible to counterattack ridicule.
Also it infuriates the opposition,
who then react to your advantage.
SAUL ALINSKY, in *Rules for Radicals* (1971)

A man is literally what he thinks,
his character being the complete sum of all his thoughts.
JAMES ALLEN, in *As a Man Thinketh* (1903)

During his first year in office (from the morning of his inauguration on Jan. 20, 2017 to exactly one year later), the searchable Twitter archive revealed that President Trump sent out 2,568 tweets, an average of just more than seven a day. If he continues at this rate for his entire presidency, his output will exceed 10,000. Because of his unprecedented use of Twitter, we have more detailed information about the thoughts of this president than any other in history—and it suggests that a man may also be known by the complete sum of all his tweets.

If one cannot command attention by one's
admirable qualities at least one can be a nuisance.
MARGERY ALLINGHAM, in *Death of a Ghost* (1934)

When people show you who they are, believe them.
MAYA ANGELOU, a signature saying, on *The Oprah Winfrey Show* (June 18, 1997)

When Winfrey told Angelou that this was one of the most important life lessons she had ever learned from her, the poet simply smiled and replied: "If a person says to you, I'm selfish, or I'm mean, or I am unkind, or I'm crazy, believe them; they know themselves much better than you do." In 2011, Winfrey replayed portions of that 1997 interview in a "Lifeclass" broadcast on the OWN. In one segment, Winfrey did her best imitation of Angelou when she recalled the poet saying:

"My dear, when people show you who they are,
why don't you believe them?
Why must you be shown twenty-nine times
before you can see who they really are?
Why can't you get it the first time?"

I distrust those people who know so well
what God wants them to do,
because I notice it always coincides with their own desires.
SUSAN B. ANTHONY, in remarks at 1896 meeting of the
National-American Woman Suffrage Association

In *Bird by Bird: Some Instructions on Writing and Life* (1994), Anne Lamott provided an updated version of Anthony's thought when she passed along a similar observation from one of her friends, a priest she affectionately calls Father Tom: "You can safely assume you've created God in your own image when it turns out that God hates all the same people you do."

It is only that my illusion is more real to me than reality.
And so do we often build our world on an error,
and cry out that the universe is falling to pieces,
if any one but lift a finger to replace the error by truth.
MARY ANTIN, in *The Promised Land* (1912)

Pay attention to your enemies,
for they are the first to discover your mistakes.
ANTISTHENES (5th c. BC), quoted in Diogenes Laërtius, *Lives
and Opinions of Eminent Philosophers* (3rd c. AD)

**Illusion is the dust the devil throws
in the eyes of the foolish.**
MINNA THOMAS ANTRIM, in *Naked Truth and Veiled Illusions* (1901)

**Show me one who boasts continually of his "openness,"
and I will show you one who conceals much.**
MINNA THOMAS ANTRIM, in *At the Sign of the Golden Calf* (1905)

Trump has boasted repeatedly about the unprecedented transparen-
cy—or openness—of his administration. His latest came in response
to a flurry of congressional subpoenas received by the White House
shortly after the Mueller report became public. In remarks to the press
on April 24, 2019, he said: "I have been the most transparent president
and administration in the history of the country by far."

**Cowards are not invariably liars,
but liars are invariably cowards.**
MINNA THOMAS ANTRIM, in *Knocks* (1905)

**Psychologically speaking, one may say
that the hypocrite is too ambitious;
not only does he want to appear virtuous before others,
he wants to convince himself.**
HANNAH ARENDT, in *On Revolution* (1963)

Earlier, Arendt introduced the thought by writing: "The hypocrite's
crime is that he bears false witness against himself."

They should rule who are able to rule best.
ARISTOTLE, in *Politics* (4th c. BC)

> **The least initial deviation from the truth**
> **is multiplied later a thousandfold.**
>
> ARISTOTLE, in On the Heavens (4th c. BC)

> **If happiness is activity in accordance with excellence,**
> **it is reasonable that it should be**
> **in accordance with the highest excellence.**
>
> ARISTOTLE, in Nichomachean Ethics (4th c. BC)

At a 1963 White House press conference less than a month before his assassination, John F. Kennedy was asked by a reporter if he enjoyed the presidency. He replied:

> "I have given before to this group the
> definition of happiness of the Greeks,
> and I will define it again: it is full use
> of your powers along lines of excellence.
> I find, therefore, the Presidency provides some happiness."

In his remark, Kennedy was inspired by a passage from Edith Hamilton's *The Greek Way* (1930): "'The exercise of vital powers along lines of excellence in a life affording them scope' is an old Greek definition of happiness." Hamilton's observation, in turn, was based on the Aristotle quotation above. This JFK anecdote is a sad reminder of the depths to which presidential rhetoric had descended. Three years into the Trump presidency, no soaring words have yet been uttered, and nothing close to eloquence has yet been witnessed.

> **Liars when they speak the truth are not believed.**
>
> ARISTOTLE, quoted in Diogenes Laërtius, Lives and Opinions of Eminent Philosophers (3rd c. AD)

There is no belief, however foolish, that will not
gather its faithful adherents who will defend it to the death.

ISAAC ASIMOV, in *The Stars in Their Courses* (1971)

There is a cult of ignorance in the United States,
and there has always been.
The strain of anti-intellectualism has been a constant thread
winding its way through our political and cultural life,
nurtured by the false notion that democracy means
that "my ignorance is just as good as your knowledge."

ISAAC ASIMOV, "A Cult of Ignorance," in *Newsweek* (Jan. 21, 1980)

He couldn't see a belt without hitting below it.

MARGOT ASQUITH, on David Lloyd George, in
The Listener (London; June 11, 1953)

Stupidity is the same as evil if you judge by the results.

MARGARET ATWOOD, in *Surfacing* (1972)

Vanity working on a weak head
produces every sort of mischief.

JANE AUSTEN, in *Emma* (1815)

The words come from Mr. Knightley as he and Emma are discussing
Harriet Smith, a seventeen-year-old beauty who'd never be mistak-
en for a deep thinker. If we apply Knightley's remark to the political
arena, the implications are clear: vanity is always problematical, but
especially with those lacking self-awareness or powers of reasoning.

How quick come the reasons for approving what we like!

JANE AUSTEN, in *Persuasion* (1818)

There are conditions
of blindness
so voluntary that
they become complicity.

Paul Bourget

**There is no such thing as a problem
without a gift for you in its hands.**
RICHARD BACH, in *Illusions: The Adventures
of a Reluctant Messiah* (1977)

**The speaking in a perpetual hyperbole
is comely in nothing but love.**
FRANCIS BACON, "Of Love," in *Essays* (1625)

While Bacon was willing to forgive extravagant exaggerations in matters of love, he considered them unseemly in other arenas, including politics. And regarding "perpetual hyperbole," no American president comes close to Donald Trump. Here's how Trump justified the behavior in his 1987 bestseller *The Art of the Deal* (through the words of ghostwriter Tony Schwartz):

> "I play to people's fantasies. People may not always think big themselves, but they can still get very excited by those who do. That's why a little hyperbole never hurts. People want to believe that something is the biggest and the greatest and the most spectacular. I call it truthful hyperbole."

Despite Trump's claims, most fact-checkers have concluded that his perpetual hyperbolic assertions contain far more fiction than truth—and they have earned him more "Pinocchios" and "Pants on Fire" designations than any other politician in history.

**Nothing doth more hurt in a state
than that cunning men must pass for wise.**
FRANCIS BACON, "Of Cunning," in *Essays* (1625)

There is no such flatterer as is a man's self.
FRANCIS BACON, "Of Friendship," in *Essays* (1625)

While we typically think of flattery as insincere or manipulative praise from others, Bacon reminds us here that *self-praise* may be the most common form of flattery (in a later essay in his book, he described self-praise as "the arch flatterer"). The phenomenon shows up most commonly in people who are so prone to singing their own praises that they are commonly dismissed as "legends in their own minds."

The less you speak of your greatness,
the more I will think of it.
FRANCIS BACON, a remark to the boastful Sir Edward Coke, in
Joseph Sortain, *The Life of Francis, Lord Bacon* (1851)

There is apparently only one trait in human nature
which is stronger than curiosity. It is credulity.
The things people will believe are unbelievable.
LOUISE MAXWELL BAKER, in *Out on a Limb* (1946)

I imagine one of the reasons
people cling to their hates so stubbornly
is because they sense, once hate is gone,
they will be forced to deal with pain.
JAMES BALDWIN, "Me and My House," in *Harper's* (Nov. 1955)

Baldwin was reflecting on his own longstanding hatred for his father. In 1943, a week before his nineteenth birthday, Baldwin returned to his Harlem home after a several-year absence to see his mother and check in on his ailing father. He wrote: "The moment I saw him I knew why I had put off this visit so long. I had told my mother that I did not want to see him because I hated him. But this was not true. It was only that I 'had' hated him and I wanted to hold on to this hatred. I did not want to look on him as a ruin; it was not a ruin I had hated." His father died a week later. It does not seem inappropriate to extend Baldwin's *cling to their hates* observation to the virulence exhibited by so many Trump supporters at those mass rallies—and it does not seem like a stretch to see that the hatred being clung to is masking a great deal of inner pain.

**People who cling to their delusions find it difficult,
if not impossible, to learn anything worth learning.**
JAMES BALDWIN, in *No Name in the Street* (1972)

**If you are to judge a man, you must know
his secret thoughts, sorrows, and feelings.**
HONORÉ DE BALZAC, in *La Peau de Chagrin* (1831)

**A man's own vanity is a swindler
that never lacks for a dupe.**
HONORÉ DE BALZAC, in *The Jealousies of a Country Town* (1838)

**Too many of our countrymen rejoice in stupidity,
look upon ignorance as a badge of honor.
They condemn everything they don't understand.**
TALLULAH BANKHEAD, in *Tallulah: My Autobiography* (1952)

**Every one that flatters thee
Is no friend in misery.**
RICHARD BARNFIELD, "Ode," in *Poems* (1596)

Barnfield, a contemporary of Shakespeare, is thought to be the "rival poet" mentioned in Shakespeare's sonnets. He went on to write:

"Every man will be thy friend
Whilst thou hast wherewith to spend;
But if store of crowns be scant,
No man will supply thy want."

People who want to share their religious views with you
almost never want you to share yours with them.
DAVE BARRY, in *Dave Barry Turns Fifty* (1998)

Criticism and dissent are
the indispensable antidote to major delusions.
ALAN BARTH, in *The Loyalty of Free Men* (1951)

Man can certainly keep on lying (and does so);
but he cannot make truth falsehood.
KARL BARTH, in *Church Dogmatics: The Doctrine of God* (1942)

That in all times, mediocrity has
dominated, that is indubitable;
but that it reigns more than ever, that it is
becoming absolutely triumphant and inhibiting,
this is what is as true as it is distressing.
CHARLES BAUDELAIRE, in "Salon of 1859" (1859)

Mediocre comes from the same root that gives us *medium,* and there is nothing inherently negative in the term (its essential meaning is similar to *average,* a middle point between high and low, small and large, or top and bottom). Yet, the term is often used to describe something or someone unsatisfactory, as in a mediocre wine or a mediocre artist. Whenever people desire excellence or greatness, they are disappointed by mediocrity—and this is true whether the subject is wine, artists, or politicians.

A proud man is seldom a grateful man,
for he never thinks he gets as much as he deserves.

HENRY WARD BEECHER, in *Life Thoughts* (1858)

Greatness lies not in being strong,
but in the right using of strength;
and strength is not used rightly when it serves
only to carry a man above his fellows
for his own solitary glory.

HENRY WARD BEECHER, in *Life Thoughts* (1858)

A noble man compares and estimates himself
by an idea which is higher than himself;
and a mean man by one which is lower than himself.
The one produces aspiration; the other, ambition.
Ambition is the way in which a vulgar man aspires.

HENRY WARD BEECHER, in *Life Thoughts* (1858)

There is nothing which vanity does not desecrate.

HENRY WARD BEECHER, in *Proverbs from Plymouth Pulpit* (1887)

If a man is great in the spiritual elements,
he is great everywhere else;
but, if he is small there, he is small everywhere else.

HENRY WARD BEECHER, in *Proverbs from Plymouth Pulpit* (1887)

What is easy to men of genius
becomes fatal to men who are without genius.

HENRY WARD BEECHER, in *Proverbs from Plymouth Pulpit* (1887)

Beecher's observation can be extended to all people who ultimately fail at something that is beyond their capabilities. Laurence J. Peter immortalized the idea in his *Peter Principle* (1969). The phenomenon has also been humorously enshrined in presidential politics, as when Rich Little said: "Jimmy Carter as president is like Truman Capote marrying Dolly Parton. The job is just too big for him." Napoleon I offered a variation on the theme, which may be summarized this way: sometimes the position doesn't diminish the person so much as the person diminishes the position.

A great deal of intelligence can be invested in ignorance when the need for illusion is great.
SAUL BELLOW, in *To Jerusalem and Back* (1976)

Secrecy is an instrument of conspiracy; it ought not, therefore, to be a system of a regular government.
JEREMY BENTHAM, "On Publicity," in *Essays on Political Tactics* (1791)

Politics and religion mixed is the headiest cocktail ever invented.
NORAH BENTINCK, in *My Wandering and Memories* (1924)

He who has the bigger stick has the better chance of imposing his definitions of reality.
PETER L. BERGER AND THOMAS LUCKMANN, in *The Social Construction of Reality* (1966)

It is impossible that a man who is false to his friends and neighbors should be true to the public.
GEORGE BERKELEY, in *Maxims Concerning Patriotism* (1750)

Ignorance is an evil weed,
which dictators may cultivate among their dupes,
but which no democracy can afford among its citizens.
WILLIAM BEVERIDGE, in *Full Employment in a Free Society* (1944)

I'm not sure what the Founding Fathers would have to say about today's "low-information voters," but I believe it would be a source of deep concern. The founders all believed that an educated citizenry was not only essential to the functioning of a democracy, but the greatest deterrent to tyranny. Thomas Jefferson expressed it well in an 1816 letter to Col. Charles Yancey: "If a nation expects to be ignorant and free…it expects what never was and never will be." In that letter, Jefferson also offered a thought about the best way to combat the evil weed of ignorance: "Where the press is free, and every man able to read, all is safe."

When an alien resides with you in your land,
you shall not oppress the alien.
The alien who resides with you shall be
to you as the citizen among you;
you shall love the alien as yourself,
for you were aliens in the land of Egypt.
THE BIBLE, Leviticus 19:33-34 (NRSV)

In my research over the past few years, I found over a hundred passages that appear relevant in any discussion of the Bible and Donald Trump. I'll present fifty of them here.

In the Leviticus passage above, I chose the translation from the *New Revised Standard Version* (NRSV) because it uses the contemporary term *alien*. The *King James Version* (KJV) and *Revised Standard Version* (RSV) use the term *stranger*, while the *New Living Translation* (NLT) employs the term *foreigner*. All, however, clearly express the injunction to extend kindness, compassion, and mercy to *the others* in our midst.

In each of the passages that follow, I will indicate which translation has been chosen.

If you fail to keep your word,
then you will have sinned against the Lord,
and you may be sure that your sin will find you out.
Numbers 32:23 (NLT)

> He that trusteth in his riches shall fall.
> Proverbs 11:28 (KJV)

The way of a fool is right in his own eyes,
but a wise man listens to advice.
Proverbs 12:15 (RSV)

> The vexation of a fool is known at once,
> but the prudent man ignores an insult.
> Proverbs 12:16 (RSV)

Before honor is humility.
Proverbs 15:33 (KJV)

> Every one who is arrogant is an abomination to the Lord;
> be assured, he will not go unpunished.
> Proverbs 16:5 (RSV)

Pride goeth before destruction,
and a haughty spirit before a fall.
Proverbs 16:18 (RSV)

> He who is slow to anger is better than the mighty,
> and he who rules his spirit than he who takes a city.
> Proverbs 16:32 (RSV)

He who mocks the poor insults his Maker;
he who is glad at calamity will not go unpunished.
Proverbs 17:5 (RSV)

> He who has knowledge spares his words,
> and a man of understanding is of a calm spirit.
> Proverbs 17:27 (NKJV)

A fool's mouth is his ruin,
and his lips are a snare to himself.
Proverbs 18:7 (RSV)

Bread gained by deceit is sweet to a man,
but afterward his mouth will be full of gravel.
Proverbs 20:17 (RSV)

A good name is rather to be chosen than great riches.
Proverbs 22:1 (KJV)

For as he thinketh in his heart, so is he:
Eat and drink, saith he to thee;
but his heart is not with thee.
Proverbs 23:7 (KJV)

For men to search their own glory is not glory.
Proverbs 25:27 (KJV)

Answer not a fool according to his folly,
lest you be like him yourself.
Proverbs 26:4 (RSV)

As a dog returneth to his vomit,
so a fool returneth to his folly.
Proverbs 26:11 (KJV)

Do you see a man who is wise in his own eyes?
There is more hope for a fool than for him.
Proverbs 26:12 (RSV)

Let another man praise thee, and not thine own mouth;
a stranger, and not thine own lips.
Proverbs 27:2 (KJV)

A fool uttereth all his mind.
Proverbs 29:11 (KJV)

Where there is no vision, the people perish.
Proverbs 29:18 (KJV)

> What sorrow for those who drag their sins
> behind them with ropes made of lies,
> who drag wickedness behind them like a cart!
> Isaiah 5:18 (NLT)

> Woe unto them that call evil good, and good evil;
> that put darkness for light, and light for darkness;
> that put bitter for sweet, and sweet for bitter!
> Isaiah 5:20 (KJV)

> What sorrow awaits the unjust judges
> and those who issue unfair laws.
> They deprive the poor of justice and deny
> the rights of the needy among my people.
> Isaiah 10:1-2 (NLT)

> I will put an end to the pride of the arrogant,
> and lay low the haughtiness of the ruthless.
> Isaiah 13:11 (RSV)

> Hear now this, O foolish people,
> and without understanding;
> which have eyes, and see not;
> which have ears, and hear not.
> Jeremiah 5:21 (KJV)

It was this *Jeremiah* passage that inspired Matthew Henry, in his famous biblical *Commentaries* (1708-1710), to write: "None so blind as those that will not see." Henry's pithy summary of the passage soon morphed into one of history's most famous—and insightful—proverbs (and one that goes a long way toward explaining what happened in the 2016 presidential election): "There are none so blind as those who will not see."

> He has showed you, O man, what is good;
> and what does the Lord require of you but to do justice,
> and to love kindness, and to walk humbly with your God?
> Micah 6:8 (RSV)

That which is crooked cannot be made straight.
Ecclesiastes 1:15 (KJV)

It was once believed that *Ecclesiastes* was written by Solomon around 950 BC, but biblical scholars are now in general agreement that it was written centuries later (450-200 BC). At around the same time—and quite independently—a strikingly similar observation was offered by the Chinese sage Mencius (372-289 BC): "Never has a man who has bent himself been able to make others straight."

The wise man's eyes are in his head;
but the fool walketh in darkness.
Ecclesiastes 2:14 (KJV)

But I say unto you, that whosoever looketh
on a woman to lust after her hath committed
adultery with her already in his heart.
Matthew 5:28 (KJV)

Beware of false prophets, who come to you in
sheep's clothing but inwardly are ravenous wolves.
You will know them by their fruits...
So, every sound tree bears good fruit,
but the bad tree bears evil fruit.
A sound tree cannot bear evil fruit,
nor can a bad tree bear good fruit...
Thus you will know them by their fruits.
Matthew 7:15-20 (RSV)

Not everyone who calls out to me,
"Lord! Lord!" will enter the Kingdom of Heaven.
Only those who actually do the will
of my Father in heaven will enter.
On Judgment Day...I will reply, "I never knew you.
Get away from me, you who break God's laws."
Matthew 7:21-23 (NLT)

And if the blind lead the blind,
both shall fall into the ditch.
Matthew 15:14 (KJV)

Whoever exalts himself will be humbled,
and whoever humbles himself will be exalted.
Matthew 23:12 (RSV)

And Jesus answered and said unto them,
Take heed that no man deceive you.
Matthew 24:4 (KJV)

For what shall it profit a man, if he shall
gain the whole world, and lose his own soul?
Mark 8:36 (KJV)

It is easier for a camel to go through the eye of a needle
than for a rich man to enter the kingdom of God.
Mark 10:25 (KJV)

For all that is secret will eventually
be brought into the open,
and everything that is concealed will be
brought to light and made known to all.
Luke 8:17 (NLT)

To whom much is given,
of him much will be required.
Luke 12:48 (RSV)

Professing themselves to be wise, they became fools.
Romans 1:22 (KJV)

You are not to associate with anyone who
claims to be a believer yet indulges in sexual sin,
or is greedy, or worships idols, or is abusive,
or is a drunkard, or cheats people.
Don't even eat with such people.
1 Corinthians 5:11 (NLT)

Love is patient and kind; love is not
jealous or boastful; it is not arrogant or rude.
Love does not insist on its own way;
it is not irritable or resentful;
it does not rejoice at wrong, but rejoices in the right.
Love bears all things, believes all things,
hopes all things, endures all things.

1 Corinthians 13:4-7 (RSV)

Let no one deceive you with empty words.

Ephesians 5:6 (RSV)

The love of money is the root of all evil.

1 Timothy 6:10 (KJV)

For men will be lovers of self, lovers of money, proud,
arrogant, abusive, disobedient to their parents, ungrateful,
unholy, inhuman, implacable, slanderers, profligates, fierce,
haters of good, treacherous, reckless, swollen with conceit,
lovers of pleasure rather than lovers of God, holding the
form of religion but denying the power of it.
Avoid such people.

2 Timothy 3:1-5 (RSV)

If you claim to be religious but don't control your tongue,
you are fooling yourself, and your religion is worthless.

James 1:26 (NLT)

Ye shall know the truth,
and the truth shall make you free.

John 8:32 (KJV)

The notion that the truth shall set people free is an enormously popular idea, but the problem throughout history is that all people tend
to believe truth is on their side. One solution to this dilemma was
expressed by Kahlil Gibran, who wrote in his 1923 classic *The Prophet*:
"Say not, 'I have found the truth,' but rather, 'I have found a truth.'"

This is not how people typically behave, however, especially when they believe they have God supporting their position. Whenever I hear someone seriously citing Jesus's words from the *John 8:32* passage above, I remind them of Herbert Agar's words on the subject, which can be found in his entry above.

He who says he is in the light
and hates his brother is in the darkness still.
1 John 2:9 (RSV)

> **But if any one has the world's goods**
> **and sees his brother in need,**
> **yet closes his heart against him,**
> **how does God's love abide in him?**
> 1 John 3:17 (RSV)

If any one says, "I love God,"
and hates his brother, he is a liar;
for he who does not love his brother whom he has seen,
cannot love God whom he has not seen.
1 John 4:20 (RSV)

For every man there is something in the
vocabulary that would stick to him like a second skin.
His enemies have only to find it.
AMBROSE BIERCE, in *The Devil's Dictionary* (1911)

This thought about name-calling—a Trump specialty—appeared in the *oleaginous* entry in Bierce's classic *Dictionary*. He began with this definition: "Oleaginous, *adj.* Oily, smooth, sleek." He then went on to add this comment:

"Disraeli once described the manner of Bishop [Samuel] Wilberforce as 'unctuous, oleaginous, saponaceous.' And the good prelate was ever afterward known as Soapy Sam. For every man there is something in the vocabulary that would stick to him like a second skin. His enemies have only to find it."

After the Civil War, Bierce was a young Union soldier who settled in San Francisco, where he became a newspaper columnist noted for his critical attacks on hypocritical clergymen, crooked politicians, and other frauds and phonies (his acerbic style earned him the nickname "Bitter Bierce"). In addition to the short story "An Occurrence at Owl Creek Bridge" (1890), his other claim to literary fame was *The Devil's Dictionary* (1911), a book of ironic observations and sardonic definitions. A number of items from the work are relevant to our present discussion:

Positive, *n*. Mistaken at the top of one's voice.

A bad workman quarrels with the man who calls him that.

Brain, *n*. An apparatus with which we think that we think.

Calamities are of two kinds: misfortune to ourselves, and good fortune to others.

Vote, *n*. The instrument and symbol of a freeman's power to make a fool of himself and a wreck of his country.

Idiot, *n*. A member of a large and powerful tribe whose influence in human affairs has always been dominant and controlling.

Politics, *n*. A strife of interests masquerading as a contest of principles. The conduct of public affairs for private advantage.

President, *n*. The leading figure in a small group of
men of whom—and of whom only—it is positively
known that immense numbers of their countrymen
did not want any of them for president.

There are people who exaggerate so much
that they can't tell the truth without lying.
JOSH BILLINGS (Henry Wheeler Shaw),
in Donald Day, *Uncle Sam's Uncle Josh* (1953)

A fool sees not the same tree that a wise man sees.
WILLIAM BLAKE, in *The Marriage of Heaven and Hell* (1790–1793)

Honor is like an island, rugged and without a beach;
once we have left it, we can never return.
NICOLAS BOILEAU, in *Satires* (1666)

A fool can always find a greater fool to admire him.
NICOLAS BOILEAU, in *L'Art poétique* (1674)

You have to love a nation that celebrates its
independence every July 4, not with a parade of guns,
tanks, and soldiers who file by the White House in a
show of strength and muscle, but by family picnics
where kids throw frisbees, the potato salad gets iffy,
and the flies die from happiness.
ERMA BOMBECK, in "At Wit's End" column (June 28, 1982)

It's much easier for me to imagine a praying murderer,
a praying prostitute, than a vain person praying.
Nothing is so at odds with prayer as vanity.

DIETRICH BONHOEFFER, a 1928 diary entry

It's very easy to overestimate
the importance of our own achievements
in comparison with what we owe to others.

DIETRICH BONHOEFFER, in *Letters and Papers from Prison* (1953)

We suffer primarily not from our vices
or our weaknesses, but from our illusions.
We are haunted, not by reality,
but by those images we have put in place of reality.

DANIEL J. BOORSTIN, in *The Image* (1961)

It is against Stupidity in every shape and form
that we have to wage our eternal battle.

WILLIAM BOOTH, in *In Darkest England, and the Way Out* (1890)

Booth, a British revivalist preacher who founded the Salvation Army
in 1878, witnessed stupidity at all social levels. He continued with a
thought that is particularly relevant to the subject we are considering here: "But how can we wonder at the want of sense on the part
of those who have had no advantages, when we see such plentiful
absence of that commodity on the part of those who have had all the
advantages?"

There are conditions of blindness so voluntary
that they become complicity.

PAUL BOURGET, in *Cosmopolis* (1892)

It is only an error in judgment to make a mistake,
but it argues an infirmity of character
to adhere to it when discovered.

CHRISTIAN NESTELL BOVEE, in *Intuitions and
Summaries of Thought* (1862)

Nobody can be kinder than the narcissist
while you react to life in his own terms.

ELIZABETH BOWEN, in *The Death of the Heart* (1938)

Life is so very simple when you have
no facts to confuse you.

PEG BRACKEN, in *A Window Over the Sink* (1981)

It isn't true, by the way, that
nothing is as bad as you think it's going to be.
Some things are exactly as bad
as you thought they were going to be,
and some things are worse.

PEG BRACKEN, in *A Window Over the Sink* (1981)

Authority without wisdom is like
a heavy axe without an edge,
fitter to bruise than polish.

ANNE BRADSTREET, in *Meditations Divine and Moral* (1664)

Truth-tellers are not always palatable.
There is a preference for candy bars.

GWENDOLYN BROOKS, in *Gottschalk and
the Grande Tarantelle* (1988)

Never underestimate the power of self-absorption.

RITA MAE BROWN, in *Starting from Scratch* (1988)

We have a large public that is very
ignorant about public affairs
and very susceptible to simplistic slogans
by candidates who appear out of nowhere,
have no track record, but mouth appealing slogans.

ZBIGNIEW BRZEZINSKI, in *The Grand Chessboard* (1997)

Nothing is so agonizing to the fine skin of vanity
as the application of a rough truth!

EDWARD GEORGE BULWER-LYTTON, in *Devereux* (1829)

No passion so effectually robs the mind
of all its powers of acting and reasoning as fear.

EDMUND BURKE, in *A Philosophical Inquiry into the Origin
of Our Ideas of the Sublime and the Beautiful* (1756)

Every demagogue in history has recognized the truth of Burke's observation, but Trump has embraced it. He begins with a conscious decision to exploit a fear (e.g., fear of immigrants) and continues with a
repetitive disinformation campaign (e.g., invading caravans of "very
bad people" marching toward the border). This activity generally
increases in the weeks before key elections, in a clear attempt to transform fear into a fever pitch of anger or outrage that is intended to
drive voters to the polls.

It is a general popular error
to imagine the loudest complainers for the public
to be the most anxious for its welfare.

EDMUND BURKE, in *Observations on a Late Publication
on the Present State of the Nation* (1769)

> He that wrestles with us
> strengthens our nerves, and sharpens our skill.
> Our antagonist is our helper.
> EDMUND BURKE, in *Reflections on the Revolution in France* (1790)

> Flattery corrupts both the receiver and the giver.
> EDMUND BURKE, in *Reflections on the Revolution in France* (1790)

No moment in the Trump presidency better exemplified this Burke observation than a June 12, 2017 White House Cabinet Meeting—the first with every member of the new cabinet present. Trump began by making a number of self-serving (and factually incorrect) remarks, including: "Never has there been a president, with few exceptions… who has passed more legislation, done more things." When he finished, Trump invited the cabinet members to introduce themselves.

You may recall seeing portions of the meeting on television, because seasoned political observers said nothing like it had ever occurred in American history. Beginning with Mike Pence, each person engaged in what can only be described as sycophantic flattery. A typical example was Chief of Staff Reince Priebus, who gushed: "On behalf of the entire senior staff around you, Mr. President, we thank you for the opportunity and blessing you've given us to serve your agenda and the American people."

In newscasts later in the day, pundits said the meeting was eerily similar to the kind of exercises in adulation they were used to seeing in North Korea and other totalitarian nations. To me, it looked like the new president not only *needed* flattery, but *expected* it. And, picking up on Burke's observation above, it was difficult to determine who was demeaned more by the exercise, the members of the cabinet, or the president.

A very great part of the mischiefs
that vex the world arises from words.
People soon forget the meaning,
but the impression and the passion remain.

EDMUND BURKE, in 1796 letter to his son Richard Burke

All men that are ruined
are ruined on the side of their natural propensities.

EDMUND BURKE, in *Two Letters on the Proposals for
Peace with the Regicide Directory* (9th ed.; 1796)

Well it is known that ambition can creep as well as soar.

EDMUND BURKE, in *Letters on a Regicide Peace* (1797)

I pick up favorite quotations,
and store them in my mind as ready armor,
offensive or defensive, amid the struggle
of this turbulent existence.

ROBERT BURNS, in letter to Mrs. Dunlop (Dec. 6, 1792)

The truest characters of ignorance
Are vanity, and pride, and arrogance.

SAMUEL BUTLER (1613–1680), in Robert Thyer, *The
Genuine Poetical Remains of Samuel Butler* (1827)

The advantage of doing one's praising for oneself is that
one can lay it on so thick and exactly in the right places.

SAMUEL BUTLER (1835-1902), in *The Way of All Flesh* (1903)

**Any man may err,
but only a fool
persists in his error.**

Marcus Tullius Cicero

Politics is not really politics any more.
It is run, for the most part, by
Madison Avenue advertising firms,
who sell politicians to the public the way
they sell bars of soap or cans of beer.

HELEN CALDICOTT, in *If You Love This Planet* (1992)

The human heart has so many crannies where vanity hides,
so many holes where falsehood works,
is so decked out with deceiving hypocrisy,
that it often dupes itself.

JOHN CALVIN, in *Institutes of the Christian Religion* (1536)

I consider looseness with words no less
of a defect than looseness of the bowels.

JOHN CALVIN, in *The Bondage and Liberation of the Will* (1543)

A man that extols himself is a fool and an idiot.

JOHN CALVIN, in *Commentary on the Epistles of Paul* (1546)

What greater vanity is there than that of
boasting without any ground for it?

JOHN CALVIN, in *Commentary on the Epistles of Paul* (1546)

Boasting about oneself, especially when there's scant evidence to back
it up, is generally considered a sign of insecurity—and a huge turn-off.
It continues to be one of the great puzzles of the 2016 presidential campaign that so many voters would overlook behavior in a presidential
candidate that they would never tolerate in a neighbor or coworker.

Hatred grows into insolence
when we desire to excel the rest of mankind
and imagine we do not belong to the common lot;
we even severely and haughtily despise
others as our inferiors.

JOHN CALVIN, in *Golden Booklet of the True Christian Life* (1551)

We should never insult others on account of their faults,
for it is our duty to show charity and respect to everyone.

JOHN CALVIN, in *Golden Booklet of the True Christian Life* (1551)

It is terrifying to see how easily,
in certain people, all dignity collapses.

ALBERT CAMUS, in *Notebooks, 1935–1942* (1952)

I love my country too much to be a nationalist.

ALBERT CAMUS, from a 1944 essay; reprinted in
Lyrical and Critical Essays (1968)

Dishonesty is the raw material not of quacks only,
but also in great part of dupes.

THOMAS CARLYLE, in "Count Cagliostro" (1833); in
Critical and Miscellaneous Essays (1839)

The greatest of faults, I should say,
is to be conscious of none.

THOMAS CARLYLE, in *On Heroes, Hero-Worship,
and the Heroic in History* (1841)

**Self-deception once yielded to,
all other deceptions follow naturally more and more.**

THOMAS CARLYLE, in *On Heroes, Hero-Worship,
and the Heroic in History* (1841)

Carlyle was writing about Napoleon I after he ascended to power. He introduced the thought by writing that Napoleon began to renounce "his old faith in Facts, took to believing in Semblances; strove to connect himself with Austrian Dynasties, Popedoms, with the old false Feudalities, which he once saw clearly to be false." As Napoleon neared the end of his reign, Carlyle wrote about him: "He did not know true from false now when he looked at them—the fearfulest [sic] penalty a man pays for yielding to untruth of heart. Self and false ambition had now become his god."

**No sadder proof can be given by a man
of his own littleness than disbelief in great men.**

THOMAS CARLYLE, in *On Heroes, Hero-Worship,
and the Heroic in History* (1841)

**"I don't think—"
"Then you shouldn't talk," said the Hatter.**

LEWIS CARROLL, in *Alice's Adventures in Wonderland* (1865)

I had long forgotten this fascinating dialogue between Alice and the Mad Hatter, and I'm not sure I would have sensed its implications for this current project except for its being featured in an anti-Trump Tweet by J. K. Rowling on May 12, 2017.

**It is a weak nation, like a weak person,
that must behave with bluster and boasting and rashness
and other signs of insecurity.**

JIMMY CARTER, in a New York City speech (Oct. 14, 1976)

Carter began by saying: "A strong nation, like a strong person, can afford to be gentle, firm, thoughtful, and restrained. It can afford to extend a helping hand to others."

> **For of all the hard things to bear and grin,**
> **The hardest is knowing you're taken in.**
> PHOEBE CARY, in "Kate Ketchem" (1873)

> **When kindness has left people, even for a few moments,**
> **we become afraid of them, as if their reason had left them.**
> WILLA CATHER, in *My Mortal Enemy* (1926)

These words come from the character Nellie Birdseye, who continues: "When it has left a place where we have always found it, it is like shipwreck; we drop from security into something malevolent and bottomless."

> **A certain combination of incompetence and indifference**
> **can cause almost as much suffering**
> **as the most acute malevolence.**
> BRUCE CATTON, in *A Stillness at Appomattox* (1953)

> **If I do not praise myself, it is because,**
> **as is commonly said, self-praise depreciates.**
> MIGUEL DE CERVANTES, in *Don Quixote* (1605)

> **Guard against that vanity which courts**
> **a compliment, or is fed by it.**
> THOMAS CHALMERS, journal entry (May 10, 1810)

Flatterers look like friends, as wolves like dogs.
GEORGE CHAPMAN, in *The Conspiracy of Byron* (1608)

"My country, right or wrong" is a thing no patriot
would ever think of saying except in a desperate case.
It is like saying, "My mother, drunk or sober."
G. K. CHESTERTON, in *The Defendant* (1901)

Evil always wins through the strength of its splendid dupes.
G. K. CHESTERTON, in *Eugenics and Other Evils* (1922)

There are two kinds of people in the world:
the conscious dogmatists and the unconscious dogmatists.
I have always found myself that
the unconscious dogmatists were by far the most dogmatic.
G. K. CHESTERTON, "On Europe and Asia," in
Generally Speaking (1928)

What embitters the world is not excess of criticism,
but absence of self-criticism.
G. K. CHESTERTON, "On Bright Old Things," in *Sidelights
on New London and Newer New York* (1932)

There is no better test of a man's ultimate chivalry
and integrity than how he behaves when he is wrong.
G. K. CHESTERTON, "The Real Dr. Johnson," in
The Common Man (1950)

If we don't believe in free expression for people we despise,
we don't believe in it at all.
NOAM CHOMSKY, in BBC-TV interview (Nov. 25, 1992)

Perhaps it is better to wake up after all, even to suffer,
rather than to remain a dupe to illusions all one's life.
KATE CHOPIN, in The Awakening (1899)

Truth, however bitter, can be accepted,
and woven into a design for living.
AGATHA CHRISTIE, Hercule Poirot speaking, in The Hollow (1946)

He sicken'd at all triumphs but his own.
CHARLES CHURCHILL, on Thomas Franklin, in The Rosciad (1761)

The force of fanatical passion is far greater
than that exerted by any philosophical belief...
It gives men something which they
think is sublime to fight for.
WINSTON CHURCHILL, in The River War (1899)

I decline utterly to be impartial
as between the fire brigade and the fire.
WINSTON CHURCHILL, in House of Commons speech (July 7, 1926)

Quotations when engraved upon the
memory give you good thoughts.
WINSTON CHURCHILL, in My Early Life (1930)

He spoke without a note, and almost without a point.
WINSTON CHURCHILL, a 1932 remark about a contemporary,
quoted in W. Manchester, The Last Lion (1988)

Criticism may not be agreeable, but it is necessary.
It fulfills the same function as pain in the human body;
it calls attention to an unhealthy state of things.
WINSTON CHURCHILL, in 1939 interview with Kingsley Martin

The interview occurred shortly after British prime minister Neville Chamberlain had disparaged critics of the government's policies as people "who foul their own nest." Churchill described the remark as "a convenient thesis, if a dangerous one." About criticism of the government, Churchill added: "If it is heeded in time, danger may be averted; if it is suppressed, a fatal distemper may develop."

An appeaser is one who feeds a crocodile
hoping it will eat him last.
WINSTON CHURCHILL, in House of Commons speech (Jan. 1940)

There have been many confusing aspects of the Trump presidency, but one of the most bewildering has been the cowardly refusal of so many Republican leaders to challenge his outrageous claims and astonishing assertions. When Trump made the completely unsubstantiated claim that he lost the 2016 popular vote to Hillary Clinton because three to five million people had voted illegally for her, only a few supporters mustered a profile in courage.

One of them was Karl Rove, who flatly declared on Fox News that "There is no evidence whatsoever" for the president's claim. Most GOP leaders, by contrast, chose the appeasement route, either remaining silent or offered namby-pamby replies. Speaker of the House Paul Ryan said he had "seen no evidence" of widespread illegal voting, but withheld comment on Trump's statement. Senate Majority Leader Mitch McConnell also refused to challenge the president, and even provided cover for him, saying about voter fraud: "It does happen. The notion that election fraud is a fiction is not true." Paul Ryan has retired and, as of this writing, the crocodile has not yet devoured Leader McConnell.

> At the bottom of all the tributes paid to democracy
> is the little man walking into the little booth,
> with a little pencil, making a little
> cross on a little bit of paper—
> no amount of rhetoric or voluminous discussion
> can possibly diminish the overwhelming
> importance of that point.
>> WINSTON CHURCHILL, in a 1944 House of Commons speech

> It would be a great reform in politics if wisdom
> could be made to spread as easily and rapidly as folly.
>> WINSTON CHURCHILL, in speech at the Guildhall (Sep. 10, 1947)

> Any man may err, but only a fool persists in his error.
>> MARCUS TULLIUS CICERO, in *Oratio Philippica I* (1st c. BC)

> There is nothing so characteristic of narrowness
> and littleness of soul as the love of riches.
>> MARCUS TULLIUS CICERO, in *De Officiis* (1st c. BC)

> The higher we are placed, the more humbly we should walk.
>> MARCUS TULLIUS CICERO, in *De Officiis* (1st c. BC)

> Where is there dignity unless there is also honesty?
>> MARCUS TULLIUS CICERO, in *Ad Atticum* (1st c. BC)

It is not easy to see how the more
extreme forms of nationalism
can long survive when men have seen
the Earth in its true perspective
as a single small globe against the stars.
ARTHUR C. CLARKE, in *The Exploration of Space* (1951)

All religions, united with government,
are more or less inimical to liberty.
All, separated from government, are compatible with liberty.
HENRY CLAY, in US House of Representatives speech (Mar. 24, 1818)

The character of a President colors his entire administration.
CLARK CLIFFORD, "The Presidency as I Have Seen It," in
Emmet John Hughes, *The Living Presidency* (1972)

By dignity I mean the absence of ludicrous
and debasing associations.
SAMUEL TAYLOR COLERIDGE, in *Biographia Literaria* (1817)

A falsehood is, in one sense, a dead thing;
but too often it moves about, galvanized by self-will,
and pushes the living out of their seats.
SAMUEL TAYLOR COLERIDGE, in *Aids to Reflection* (1825)

In politics, what begins in fear usually ends in folly.
SAMUEL TAYLOR COLERIDGE, journal entry (Oct. 5, 1830)

To most men, experience is like the stern lights of a ship,
which illumine only the track it has passed.
SAMUEL TAYLOR COLERIDGE, in an 1820 letter to a friend

In an 1831 *Table Talk* entry, Coleridge reprised the theme, and this later version went on to become one of his most famous observations: "If men could learn from history, what lessons it might teach us! But passion and party blind our eyes, and the light which experience gives is a lantern on the stern, which shines only on the waves behind us."

Vanity is a strong temptation to lying;
it makes people magnify their merit,
over-flourish their family, and
tell strange stories of their interest and acquaintance.

JEREMY COLLIER, in *Pearls of Great Price* (1838)

Riches may enable us to confer favors,
but to confer them with propriety and grace
requires a something that riches cannot give.

CHARLES CALEB COLTON, in *Lacon* (1820)

Nothing so completely baffles one who
is full of trick and duplicity himself than
straightforward and simple integrity in another.

CHARLES CALEB COLTON, in *Lacon* (1820)

If our democracy is to flourish, it must have criticism;
if our government is to function it must have dissent.

HENRY STEELE COMMAGER, in *Freedom, Loyalty, Dissent* (1954)

If names be not correct,
language is not in accordance with the truth of things.
If language be not in accordance with the truth of things,
affairs cannot be carried on to success.

CONFUCIUS, in *Analects* (6th c. BC)

The facts about the life of the ancient eastern thinker known in the West as Confucius are sketchy, but historians have long agreed that his original goal was to find a Chinese prince who would heed his advice about how to govern (the historian Will Durant called him "the sage in search of a state"). He failed in this quest, however, and in his later years resigned himself to teaching young students. His pupils went on to immortalize their teacher by recording his responses to their questions, often beginning their remembrances with the now-classic phrase, "Confucius say..." His thoughts and observations have been preserved for centuries in the *Analects,* a word that is roughly similar to the English word *sayings.*

Many of his students went on to become high government officials and advisers to Chinese rulers, thus helping Confucius posthumously achieve his lifelong dream. His influence in Chinese government went on to last more than 2,000 years, and many of his sayings now enjoy a kind of immortality. Many also speak directly to a Trump presidency, including the observation above that language must be in accordance with the truth. The following also seem relevant to our current discussion:

A man simply cannot conceal himself.

When you have faults, do not fear to abandon them.

The superior man is distressed by his want of ability.

Real knowledge is to know
the extent of one's own ignorance.

If you see what is right and fail to act on it, you lack courage.

Worry not that no one knows of you;
seek to be worth knowing.

A man who knows he has committed a mistake
and doesn't correct it is committing another mistake.

In archery we have something
like the way of the superior man.
When the archer misses the center of the target,
he turns round and seeks for the cause
of his failure in himself.

It is the way of the superior man
to prefer the concealment of his virtue,
while it daily becomes more illustrious,
and it is the way of the mean man to seek notoriety,
while he daily goes more and more to ruin.

Honor is the presence of God in man.
PAT CONROY, in *The Lords of Discipline* (1980)

These words come from the character General Bentley Durrell, who preceded the observation by saying: "I have never had to look up a definition of honor. I knew instinctively what it was. It is something I had the day I was born, and I never had to question where it came from or by what right it was mine. If I was stripped of my honor, I would choose death as certainly and unemotionally as I clean my shoes in the morning."

The narcissist enjoys being looked at and not looking back.
MASON COOLEY, in *City Aphorisms* (1986)

**Your ability to rationalize your own bad deeds
makes you believe that the whole
world is as amoral as you are.**
DOUGLAS COUPLAND, in *Shampoo Planet* (1992)

In the last analysis,
what we are communicates far more
eloquently and persuasively
than what we say or even anything we do.
STEPHEN R. COVEY, in *Principle-Centered Leadership* (1992)

If a man is vain, flatter. If timid, flatter. If boastful, flatter.
In all history, too much flattery never lost a gentleman.
KATHRYN CRAVENS, in *Pursuit of Gentlemen* (1951)

Whenever we confront an unbridled desire
we are surely in the presence of a tragedy-in-the-making.
QUENTIN CRISP, in *Manners from Heaven* (1984)

Once you are thought selfish,
not only are you forgiven a life designed
mainly to suit yourself,
which in anyone else would appear monstrous,
but if an impulse to generosity should
by chance overpower you,
you will get five times the credit of some poor selfless soul
who has been oozing kindness for years.
AMANDA CROSS (pen name of Carolyn G. Heilbrun),
in *The Question of Max* (1976)

**He who
thinks little,
errs much.**

Leonardo da Vinci

Man hoards himself when he has nothing to give away.
EDWARD DAHLBERG, in *Reasons of the Heart* (1965)

**The one pervading evil of democracy
is the tyranny of the majority,
or rather of that party, not always the majority,
that succeeds, by force or fraud, in carrying elections.**
JOHN DALBERG (Lord Acton), in *The Quarterly Review* (Jan. 1878)

**There is no worse heresy than that
the office sanctifies the holder of it.**
JOHN DALBERG (Lord Acton), in letter to
Mandell Creighton (Apr. 5, 1887)

This was the concluding line to one of history's most famous passages:
"Power tends to corrupt and absolute power corrupts absolutely. Great
men are almost always bad men, even when they exercise influence
and not authority: still more when you superadd [sic] the tendency or
the certainty of corruption by authority."

**At every step [throughout history] we are met by arguments
which go to excuse, to palliate, to confound right and wrong,
and reduce the just man to the level of the reprobate.
The men who plot to baffle and resist us are, first of all,
those who made history what it has become.**
JOHN DALBERG (Lord Acton), "Lecture on the
Study of History" (June 11, 1895)

**Judge talent at its best and character at its worst;
suspect power more than vice.**
JOHN DALBERG (Lord Acton), "Lecture on the
Study of History" (June 11, 1895)

He is loyal to his own career
but only incidentally to anything or anyone else.
HUGH DALTON, on a contemporary, in a diary entry (Sep. 17, 1941)

The world is made up for the most part
of morons and natural tyrants,
sure of themselves, strong in their
own opinions, never doubting anything.
CLARENCE DARROW, in *Personal Liberty* (1928)

Nothing so soon destroys freedom
as cowardly and servile acquiescence.
CLARENCE DARROW, in *The Story of My Life* (1932)

Darrow preceded the thought by writing: "Nothing is so loved by tyrants as obedient subjects."

When I was a boy I was told
that anybody could become President.
I'm beginning to believe it.
CLARENCE DARROW, quoted in Irving Stone,
Clarence Darrow for the Defense (1941)

Ignorance more frequently begets
confidence than does knowledge
CHARLES DARWIN, in *The Descent of Man* (1872)

The phenomenon described by Darwin in this observation occupies such a familiar place in the human experience that psychologists have a name for it: the Dunning-Kruger Effect (named after psychologists David Dunning and Justin Kruger, who introduced it in a 1999 journal article whose title says it all):

"Unskilled and Unaware of It:
How Difficulties in Recognizing One's Own Incompetence
Lead to Inflated Self-Assessments"

The problem has been recorded throughout history, as we see in Shakespeare's "The fool doth think he is wise" and similar sayings. When Donald Trump began making claims like, "I know more than the generals," psychologists around the world began to regard him as a textbook example of the Dunning-Kruger Effect, which is technically described as a *cognitive bias* in which people who lack self-awareness mistakenly harbor illusions of superior functioning in exactly those areas in which they are deficient.

**The world is full of people whose
notion of a satisfactory future is,
in fact, a return to the idealized past.**
ROBERTSON DAVIES, in *A Voice From the Attic* (1960)

He who thinks little, errs much.
LEONARDO DA VINCI, in *The Notebooks of
Leonardo da Vinci* (c. 1500)

**To speak well of a base man is much the same
as speaking ill of a good man.**
LEONARDO DA VINCI, in The *Notebooks of
Leonardo da Vinci* (c. 1500)

It's hard to escape the conclusion that Trump "has a thing" for autocratic world leaders. In addition to his bromances with Vladimir Putin and Kim Jong Un, he's had kind things to say about Philippine strongman Rodrigo Duterte, president Erdogan of Turkey, and Syrian president Bashar al-Assad.

You do ill if you praise, but worse
if you censure what you do not understand.

LEONARDO DA VINCI, in *The Notebooks of
Leonardo da Vinci* (c. 1500)

The sage was not unaware that
boldness may be the result of ignorance
as well as of knowledge,
that it may be madness and folly instead
of clear sanity and wisdom.

MILES MENANDER DAWSON, on Confucius, in
The Ethics of Confucius (1915)

In the second century BC, the Roman writer Terence famously wrote: "Fortune favors the bold." His observation quickly took hold and, a few centuries later, Cicero was describing the saying as "an old proverb." Ever since, boldness has been closely associated with courage and leadership. The Dawson observation above, however, is a nice reminder that boldness is not always a desirable thing—and can even stem from ignorance or folly. Francis Bacon also sensed the dual nature of boldness in a 1625 essay, describing it as of utmost importance in business and civil matters while also being, at times, "a child of ignorance and baseness."

In every age it has been the tyrant,
the oppressor, and the exploiter
who has wrapped himself in the cloak
of patriotism, or religion, or both
to deceive and overawe the People.

EUGENE V. DEBS, in speech in Canton, Ohio (June 16, 1918)

Duplicity is a mark of second-rate ability.
LUC DE CLAPIERS (Marquis de Vauvenargues), in
Reflections and Maxims (1746)

Nature has left this tincture in the blood,
That all men wou'd be tyrants if they cou'd.
DANIEL DEFOE, in *The History of the Kentish Petition* (1701)

The fool shouts loudly, thinking to impress the world.
MARIE DE FRANCE, in J. Barr, *Medieval Fables*
of Marie de France (1981)

Patriotism is when love of
your own people comes first;
nationalism, when hate for people
other than your own comes first.
CHARLES DE GAULLE, quoted in *Life* (May 9, 1969)

Nobody who is Somebody looks down on anybody.
MARGARET DELAND, in *Captain Archer's Daughter* (1932)

There are some people who never acknowledge
themselves in the wrong; God help them!
MADAME DE SÉVIGNÉ, in a 1689 letter

Self-love, so sensitive in its own cause,
has rarely any sympathy to spare for others.
GERMAINE DE STAËL, in *Corinne* (1807)

The real cause, the effective one, that makes men lose power
is that they have become unworthy to exercise it.

ALEXIS DE TOCQUEVILLE, in *Recollections: The
French Revolution of 1848* (1893)

You can't divide the country up into sections
and have one rule for one section and one rule for another,
and you can't encourage people's prejudices.
You have to appeal to people's best instincts,
not their worst ones.
You may win an election or so by doing the other,
but it does a lot of harm to the country.

THOMAS E. DEWEY, quoted in Merle Miller, *Plain Speaking:
An Oral Biography of Harry S Truman* (1974)

Reality is that which when you stop believing in it,
it doesn't go away.

PHILIP K. DICK, in *Valis* (1981)

I have known a vast quantity of nonsense
talked about bad men not looking you in the face.
Don't trust that conventional idea.
Dishonesty will stare honesty out of countenance,
any day in the week, if there is anything to be got by it.

CHARLES DICKENS, "Hunted Down," in *The
New York Ledger* (Aug.-Sep. 1859)

We swallow greedily any lie that flatters us,
but we sip only little by little at a truth we find bitter.

DENIS DIDEROT, in *Rameau's Nephew* (1762)

When we start deceiving ourselves into thinking
not that we want something or need something,
not that it is a pragmatic necessity for us to have it,
but that it is a *moral imperative* that we have it,
then is when we join the fashionable madmen...
and then is when we are in bad trouble.

JOAN DIDION, in *Slouching Towards Bethlehem* (1968)

No government can be long secure
without a formidable Opposition.

BENJAMIN DISRAELI, in *Coningsby* (1844)

To be conscious that you are ignorant
is a great step to knowledge.

BENJAMIN DISRAELI, in *Sybil* (1845)

It is easier to be critical than correct.

BENJAMIN DISRAELI, in an 1860 House of Commons speech

Every one likes flattery;
and when you come to Royalty you
should lay it on with a trowel.

BENJAMIN DISRAELI, an 1880 remark to Matthew Arnold

The notion that flattery can be laid on thick and heavy, as opposed to
lightly and delicately, is a masonry metaphor that emerged in England
in the 1500s. William Shakespeare gave the fledgling metaphor a major
boost when he had the character Celia say in *As You Like It* (1599):
"Well said; that was laid on with a trowel."

The president we get is the country we get.
With each new president the nation is conformed spiritually.

E. L. DOCTOROW, "The Character of Presidents,"
in *The Nation* (Nov. 9, 1992)

Doctorow continued: "He is the artificer of our malleable national soul. He proposes not only the laws but the kinds of lawlessness that governs our lives and invoke our responses. The people he appoints are cast in his image. The trouble they get into, and get us into, is his characteristic trouble. Finally, the media amplify his character into our moral weather report. He becomes the face of our sky, the conditions that prevail. One four-year-term may find us at reasonable peace with one another, working things out, and the next, trampling on each other for our scraps of bread."

If you want to be respected by others
the great thing is to respect yourself.
Only by that, only by self-respect
will you compel others to respect you.

FYODOR DOSTOEVSKY, in *The Insulted and Injured* (1861)

A man who lies to himself and listens
to his own lie comes to a point
where he does not discern any truth either
in himself or anywhere around him
and thus falls into disrespect towards himself and others.

FYODOR DOSTOEVSKY, in *The Brothers Karamazov* (1861)

These words come from a spiritual adviser named Father Zosima, who is replying to a question from the patriarch of the Karamazov family about what he needs to do to inherit eternal life. After continuing with a few more thoughts on the problem of lying to oneself, Father Zosima concludes with words that could easily have been written by a contemporary political pundit about Donald Trump:

> "A man who lies to himself is often the first to take offense.
> It sometimes feels very good to take offense, doesn't it?
> And surely he knows that no one has offended him, and
> that he himself has invented the offense and told lies just
> for the beauty of it, that he has exaggerated for the sake of
> effect, that he has picked on a word and made a mountain
> out of a pea—he knows all of that, and still he is the first
> to take offense, he likes feeling offended, it gives him great
> pleasure, and thus he reaches the point of real hostility."

If this is the first time you are reading this remarkable Dostoevsky passage, you should know that I discussed it in a bit more detail in the Introduction to this book.

I should dearly love that the world
should be ever so little better for my presence.
Even on this small stage we have our two sides,
and something might be done by throwing all one's weight
on the scale of breadth, tolerance, charity,
temperance, peace, and kindliness to man and beast.
We can't all strike very big blows,
and even the little ones count for something.
ARTHUR CONAN DOYLE, in *The Stark Munro Letters* (1895)

The words come from J. Stark Munro, the twenty-five-year-old protagonist of a heavily autobiographical novel consisting entirely of twelve lengthy letters written by Munro to a friend. The novel is one of Doyle's lesser-known works, but it is also one of his most interesting, for it provides an intimate look into his life as an aspiring physician, well before his writing career and ultimate fame as the creator of Sherlock Holmes. The entire sentiment is a beautiful *personal credo* statement, and the last line in particular encapsulates my own feelings about this book.

Throughout my life, I have seen narrow-shouldered men,
without a single exception,
committing innumerable stupid acts,
brutalizing their fellows, and perverting souls by all means.
They call the motive for their actions fame.
ISIDORE LUCIEN DUCASSE, writing under the pen name Comte
de Lautréamont, in *Les Chants de Maldoror* (1870)

What distresses me is to see that human genius
has limits and human stupidity none.
ALEXANDRE DUMAS, fils, in *Larousse's Great*
Universal Dictionary (1865)

This appears to be history's first observation suggesting that genius (or intelligence) is limited, while stupidity knows no limits. The idea has been repeated many times over the years, as when Elbert Hubbard wrote in a 1906 issue of *The Philistine*: "Genius may have its limitations, but stupidity is not thus handicapped."

To speak ill of others is a dishonest
way of praising ourselves;
Let us be above such transparent egotism.
WILL DURANT, quoted in *The New York World-*
Telegram (June 6, 1958)

The discipline of desire is the backbone of character.
WILL AND ARIEL DURANT, in *The Age of Louis XIV* (1963)

It may be true, as Lincoln supposed, that
"You can't fool all the people all the time,"
but you can fool enough of them to rule a large country.

WILL AND ARIEL DURANT, in *The Lessons of History* (1968)

Inquiry is fatal to certainty.

WILL AND ARIEL DURANT, in *The Age of Napoleon* (1975)

Power dements even more than it corrupts.

WILL AND ARIEL DURANT, in *The Age of Napoleon* (1975)

Journalism without a moral position is impossible.
Every journalist is a moralist. It's absolutely unavoidable.
A journalist is someone who looks at
the world and the way it works,
someone who takes a close look at things every day
and reports what she sees...for others.
She cannot do her work without judging what she sees.

MARGUERITE DURAS, in Foreword to
Outside: Selected Writings (1984)

**No change
of circumstances
can repair a
defect of character.**

Ralph Waldo Emerson

Given a little power over another,
little natures swell to hideous proportions.

AMELIA EARHART, in letter to her sister Muriel (Jan. 31, 1937)

I regret nothing, says arrogance.

MARIE VON EBNER-ESCHENBACH, in *Aphorisms* (1880)

When Marie Dubsky was born in 1830 (in what is now the Czech
Republic), her father, a scion of an aristocratic Moravian family, was
committed to something rare at the time: providing his daughter with
a full, classical education. When Marie was an infant, her mother died
unexpectedly, but Count Dubsky made sure that his second (and then
his third) wife hired tutors to fulfill his mission.

In 1848, at age 18, Marie married her cousin, the Austrian Field
Marshall Baron Moritz von Ebner-Eschenbach. She seemed destined
for an aristocratic life, but, over the objections of her husband, attempted a literary career instead. After an unsuccessful attempt at playwrit-
ing, she was inspired by the works of Ivan Turgenev to write what
we would now call psychological novels. Her many novels became
popular throughout Europe, and she is now considered an important
nineteenth century Austrian-German writer.

In 1880, a collection of her personal observations was published in
German under the title *Aphorismen* (it appeared in English as *Aphorisms*
in 1892). If a great aphorist is one who captures truths about the human
experience in a succinct and memorable way, then Ebner-Eschenbach
ranks as one of the great masters of the form. Many of her creations—
like the observation above about arrogant people feeling no regret—
have a definite Trump "feel" about them. Here are some others that
also seem to apply:

Conquer, but never triumph.

Privilege is the greatest enemy of justice.

To have and not to give is often worse than to steal.

What you wish to do you are apt to think you ought to do.

"It is impossible to help all," says the miser, and—helps none.

We are so vain that we care even for the
opinion of those we don't care for.

The little bit of truth contained in many
a lie is what makes them so terrible.

Whoso appears before the public should
expect no consideration and demand none.

The mediocre always feel as if they're fighting
for their lives when confronted by the excellent.

Have patience with the quarrelsomeness of the stupid.
It is not easy to comprehend that one does not comprehend.

★ ★ ★

Great mischief comes from attempts to
steady other people's altars.
MARY BAKER EDDY, "Wedlock," in *Miscellaneous
Writings, 1883-1896* (1896)

Never let us confuse what is legal with what is right.
MARIAN WRIGHT EDELMAN, in "Call to Renewal"
Speech (Chicago; Sep. 14, 1996)

Edelman was speaking about a Republican-drafted welfare reform bill
that had just been signed into law by President Clinton (she described
the event as "a moral blot" on his presidency). She added after the

foregoing observation: "Everything Hitler did in Nazi Germany was legal, but it was not right."

**Enough committed fleas biting strategically
can make even the biggest dog uncomfortable
and transform even the biggest nation.**
MARIAN WRIGHT EDELMAN, a 1980 remark, quoted in The Children
Defense Fund's *The State of America's Children* (1991)

**An inaccurate use of words produces
such a strange confusion in all reasoning that
in the heat of debate, the combatants, unable to distinguish
their friends from their foes, fall promiscuously on both.**
MARIA EDGEWORTH, in *Letters of Julia and Caroline* (1795)

The character Caroline continued: "A skillful disputant knows well how to take advantage of this confusion, and sometimes endeavors to create it." This observation from Edgeworth reminded me that, despite his many flaws, Trump has some unique strengths. One of them is that he is a crafty and *skillful disputant*, difficult to pin down in an interview and almost impossible to defeat in a debate.

**Tyranny and injustice always produce
cunning and falsehood.**
MARIA EDGEWORTH, "Lame Jervas," in *Popular Tales* (1804)

**Persons not habituated to reason
often argue absurdly, because,
from particular instances, they deduce general conclusions,
and extend the result of their limited experience
of individuals indiscriminately to whole classes.**
MARIA EDGEWORTH, in *Ennui* (1809)

We are all apt to think that an opinion
that differs from our own is a prejudice.

MARIA EDGEWORTH, in *Belinda* (1811)

Every man who takes a part in politics,
especially in times when parties run high,
must expect to be abused: they must bear it;
and their friends must learn to bear it for them.

MARIA EDGEWORTH, in *Ormond* (1817)

No matter that patriotism is too often
the refuge of scoundrels.
Dissent, rebellion, and all-around hell-raising
remain the true duty of patriots.

BARBARA EHRENREICH, in *The Worst Years of Our Lives* (1990)

The odd thing is that the right, even when it is in power,
likes to think of itself as an embattled minority
against this elite that somehow runs everything.

BARBARA EHRENREICH, in *Talking About a Revolution* (1998)

The premise that the elites run everything, long a mantra among right-wing Republicans, was brilliantly seized upon by candidate Trump—and it made it so much easier for primary voters to embrace him as a fellow victim of a rigged system. Trump continued to play the victim role throughout his presidency, once even saying (in typical hyperbolic fashion): "No politician in history—and I say this with great surety—has been treated worse or more unfairly." A November 2017 *Atlantic* article was appropriately titled: "America's Victim in Chief."

Nationalism is an infantile disease.
It is the measles of mankind.

ALBERT EINSTEIN, in interview in *The Saturday*
Evening Post (Oct. 26, 1929)

Measles is a childhood disease, and Einstein's metaphor suggests that nationalism is an immature, simplistic, and even infantile, kind of thinking—more understandable centuries ago, perhaps, but increasingly inappropriate in modern times.

Desire for approval and recognition is a healthy motive;
but the desire to be acknowledged as better, stronger,
or more intelligent...easily leads to an excessively
egoistic psychological adjustment, which may become
injurious for the individual and for the community.

ALBERT EINSTEIN, in a 1936 speech in Albany, New York

Whoever is careless with truth in small matters
cannot be trusted in important affairs.

ALBERT EINSTEIN, in remarks at Centennial
Symposium in Jerusalem (1979)

Belligerence is the hallmark of insecurity—
the secure nation does not need threat
to maintain its position.

DWIGHT D. EISENHOWER, in Allan Taylor,
What Eisenhower Thinks (1952)

If a political party does not have its foundation in
the determination to advance a cause
that is right and that is moral,
then it is not a political party; it is merely
a conspiracy to seize power.

DWIGHT D. EISENHOWER, in address at Republican
Women's National Conference (Mar. 6, 1956)

You do not lead by hitting people over the head—
that's assault, not leadership.

DWIGHT D. EISENHOWER

This is the way the quotation is almost always presented, but it's a slightly abridged version of Eisenhower's original words, which were first quoted in *The Ordeal of Power: A Political Memoir of the Eisenhower Years* (1963), by Emmet John Hughes:

> "Now, look, I happen to know a little about leadership. I've had to work with a lot of nations, for that matter, at odds with each other. And I tell you this: you do not lead by hitting people over the head. Any damn fool can do that, but it's usually called 'assault'—not 'leadership.'"

In order to be a leader, a man must have followers;
to have followers, a leader must have their confidence.
Hence the supreme quality for a leader
is unquestionably integrity.
Without it no real success is possible,
no matter whether it is on a section gang,
a football field, in an army, or in an office.

DWIGHT D. EISENHOWER, in Clarence Poe,
My First Eighty Years (1963)

Eisenhower continued: "If a man's associates find him guilty of pho-
niness, if they find that he lacks forthright integrity, he will fail. His
teachings and actions must square with each other. The first great
need, therefore, is integrity and high purpose."

**A man can never do anything at
variance with his own nature.**
GEORGE ELIOT, in *Adam Bede* (1859)

**He was like a cock,
who thought the sun had risen to hear him crow.**
GEORGE ELIOT, in *Adam Bede* (1859)

This is how the quotation is usually presented, and it nicely captures
the essence of self-absorbed and self-aggrandizing individuals. The
full passage in which the observation originally appeared is even more
interesting, though, and I thought you might appreciate the backstory.
As Mr. and Mrs. Irwine discuss Mrs. Poyser, he says with admiration:

> "Her tongue is like a new-set razor. She's quite original in
> her talk, too; one of those untaught wits that help to stock a
> country with proverbs. I told you the capital thing I heard
> her say about Craig—that he was like a cock, who thought
> the sun had risen to hear him crow. Now, that's an Aesop's
> fable in a sentence."

**A fool or an idiot is one who
expects things to happen that never can happen.**
GEORGE ELIOT, in *Felix Holt, the Radical* (1866)

There is hardly any mental misery worse
than that of having our own serious phrases,
our own rooted beliefs,
caricatured by a charlatan or a hireling.

GEORGE ELIOT, in *Felix Holt, the Radical* (1866)

Character is not cut in marble—
it is not something solid and unalterable.
It is something living and changing,
and may become diseased as our bodies do.

GEORGE ELIOT, in *Middlemarch* (1871-72)

It is a common sentence that Knowledge is power;
but who hath duly considered or
set forth the power of Ignorance?
Knowledge slowly builds up what
Ignorance in an hour pulls down.

GEORGE ELIOT, in *Daniel Deronda* (1874)

Eliot continued: "Knowledge, through patient and frugal centuries,
enlarges discovery and makes record of it; Ignorance wanting its day's
dinner, lights a fire with the record, and gives a flavor to its one roast
with the burnt souls of many generations." A year later, in *The Inn
Album* (1875), Robert Browning would express a similar idea, but far
more succinctly: "Ignorance is not innocence, but sin."

Ignorance gives one a large range of probabilities.

GEORGE ELIOT, in *Daniel Deronda* (1874)

No evil dooms us hopelessly except the evil we love,
and desire to continue in, and make no effort to escape from.

GEORGE ELIOT, in *Daniel Deronda* (1876)

As to memory, it is known that this frail faculty
naturally lets drop the facts which are
less flattering to our self-love—
when it does not retain them carefully
as subjects not to be approached,
marshy spots with a warning flag over them.

GEORGE ELIOT, in *Impressions of Theophrastus Such* (1879)

There are two complete thoughts here, both interesting. The first is that we tend to forget things that are inconsistent with—or worse, unflattering to—the way we view ourselves. The second is *interpersonal* in nature: when we do remember the less flattering things about ourselves, other people are taking a risk when they bring them to our attention.

Co-dependence...taking someone
else's temperature to see how you feel.

LINDA ELLERBEE, in *Move On* (1991)

I consider this *the single best thing ever said* on codependency, and it perfectly describes the behavior of so many Republicans—leaders as well as rank-and-file—who were extremely reluctant to take a position on a subject until after Trump weighed in on it.

When a whole country is roaring
Patriotism at the top of its voice,
I am fain to explore the
cleanliness of its hands & purity of its heart.

RALPH WALDO EMERSON, journal entry (Dec. 10, 1824)

Nature delights in punishing stupid people.

RALPH WALDO EMERSON, a journal entry (July 9, 1839)

> **If the hive be disturbed by rash and stupid hands,
> instead of honey, it will yield us bees.**
>
> RALPH WALDO EMERSON, "Prudence," in *Essays: First Series* (1841)

> **Every violation of truth
> is not only a sort of suicide in the liar,
> but is a stab at the health of human society.**
>
> RALPH WALDO EMERSON, "Prudence," in *Essays: First Series* (1841)

> **A great man is always willing to be little.**
>
> RALPH WALDO EMERSON, "Compensation," in
> *Essays: First Series* (1841)

> **No change of circumstances
> can repair a defect of character.**
>
> RALPH WALDO EMERSON, "Character," in
> *Essays: Second Series* (1844)

> **In failing circumstances no man
> can be relied on to keep his integrity.**
>
> RALPH WALDO EMERSON, "Wealth," in *The Conduct of Life* (1860)

Before Trump won the 2016, election, he threw out a number of suggestions that he might not "accept" the verdict because the system was "rigged" or the results might be invalid because of massive voter fraud. If Trump finds himself in "failing circumstances" at the conclusion of the 2020 presidential election—especially if the contest is a squeaker—we can expect a barrage of fanciful and downright false claims, a further erosion of trust in our American institutions, and a possible constitutional crisis.

People seem not to see that their opinion of the world
is also a confession of character.
RALPH WALDO EMERSON, "Worship," in *The Conduct of Life* (1860)

Great men...have not been boasters and buffoons.
RALPH WALDO EMERSON, "Fate," in *The Conduct of Life* (1860)

The louder he talked of his honor,
the faster we counted our spoons.
RALPH WALDO EMERSON, "Fate," in *The Conduct of Life* (1860)

What you *are* stands over you...and thunders so
that I cannot hear what you say to the contrary.
RALPH WALDO EMERSON, in *Letters and Social Aims* (1875)

In the last analysis all tyranny rests on fraud,
on getting someone to accept false assumptions.
Any man who for one moment
abandons or suspends the questioning spirit
has for that moment betrayed humanity.
BERGAN EVANS, in *The Natural History of Nonsense* (1946)

**If you love
yourself too much,
nobody else will
love you at all.**

Thomas Fuller, MD

What we do stems directly from what we believe.
> MILLICENT FENWICK, in *Vogue's Book of Etiquette* (1948)

**The bully must be met with instant repulse
or he multiplies his own violence.
A placated bully is a hand-fed bully.**
> EDNA FERBER, in *A Kind of Magic* (1963)

A bit later in her autobiography, Ferber went on to add: "One thing I've learned in life; you cannot placate the power-mad. You must—to paraphrase an old saying—take the bully by the horns. Early."

**Democracy no longer works for the poor
if politicians treat them as a separate race.**
> FRANK FIELD, in *The Independent* (London; Oct. 29, 1994)

I never vote for anybody, I always vote against.
> W. C. FIELDS, quoted in Robert Lewis Taylor,
> *W. C. Fields, His Follies, His Fortunes* (1949)

**It is an easy thing to call names;
any fool is equal to that.**
> MARTHA FINLEY, in *Elsie's Motherhood* (1876)

In Finley's novel, the character Mr. Leland says this to Mr. Dinsmore, who replies: "True; and the weapon of vituperation is generally used by those who lack brains for argument or are upon the wrong side."

**Nothing is more humiliating than to see
idiots succeed in enterprises we have failed in.**
> GUSTAVE FLAUBERT, in *Sentimental Education* (1869)

It's so much easier to suggest solutions
when you don't know too much about the problem.

MALCOLM FORBES, in *The Sayings of Chairman Malcolm* (1978)

Are you not justified in feeling inferior,
when you seek to cover it up
with arrogance and insolence?

MALCOLM FORBES, in a 1994 issue of *Forbes*

A person completely wrapped up in himself
makes a small package.

HARRY EMERSON FOSDICK, in *On Being a Real Person* (1943)

Men are not against you;
they are merely for themselves.

GENE FOWLER, in *Skyline* (1961)

The Praise you take, altho' it be your Due,
Will be suspected if it come from you.

BENJAMIN FRANKLIN, in *Poor Richard's Almanack* (Sep. 1757)

Benjamin Franklin came out with the first edition of *Poor Richard's Almanack* in 1732 and continued to publish new editions every year for the next twenty-five years. Each edition provided weather forecasts, household hints, astrological and astronomical information, mathematical puzzles, predictions of upcoming events, and, of course, "Poor Richard's" sayings and aphorisms (some of which were original to Franklin and others which borrowed heavily from—or directly plagiarized—English and European writers). The *Almanack*, as much as any other publication, helped instill a constellation of core values in a new American nation that was developing an identity uniquely its own. Below are some additional Poor Richard sayings that apply to our current topic:

He does not possess Wealth, it possesses him. (1734)

Who has deceiv'd thee so oft as thyself? (1738)

There is much difference between imitating
a good man, and counterfeiting him. (1738)

Search others for their virtues, thy self for thy vices. (1738)

None but the well-bred man knows how to
confess a fault or acknowledge himself in error. (1738)

He that falls in love with himself, will have no Rivals. (1739)

There are lazy Minds as well as lazy Bodies. (1740)

A Flatterer never seems absurd:
The Flatter'd always takes his Word. (1740)

Best is the Tongue that feels the rein—
He that talks much, must talk in vain. (1741)

Pardoning the Bad is injuring the Good. (1748)

The first Degree of Folly is
to conceit one's self wise;
the second to profess it;
the third to despise Counsel. (1754)

You may give a Man an Office, but
you cannot give him Discretion. (1754)

Being Ignorant is not so much a Shame,
as being unwilling to learn. (1755)

Love your Enemies, for they tell you your Faults. (1756)

They that won't be counselled,
can't be helped. (1758)

Just as love for one individual
which excludes the love for others is not love,
love for one's country which is not
part of one's love for humanity is not love,
but idolatrous worship.

ERICH FROMM, in *The Sane Society* (1955)

Narcissism is the earliest stage of human development,
and the person who in later life
has returned to this stage is incapable of love.

ERICH FROMM, in *The Art of Loving* (1956)

The narcissistic orientation is one
in which one experiences as real
only that which exists within oneself,
while the phenomena in the outside world
have no reality in themselves,
but are experienced only from the viewpoint
of their being useful or dangerous to one.

ERICH FROMM, in *The Art of Loving* (1956)

Fromm continued: "The opposite pole to narcissism is objectivity; it is the faculty to see other people and things as they are, objectively, and to be able to separate this objective picture from a picture which is formed by one's desires and fears."

Be you never so high, the law is above you.

THOMAS FULLER, MD, in *Gnomologia* (1732)

Envy shooteth at others and woundeth herself.

THOMAS FULLER, MD, in *Gnomologia* (1732)

He that hath the worst cause makes the most noise.

THOMAS FULLER, MD, in *Gnomologia* (1732)

**If you love yourself too much,
nobody else will love you at all.**

THOMAS FULLER, MD, in *Gnomologia* (1732)

**Religion is the best Armor in the World,
but the worst Cloak.**

THOMAS FULLER, MD, in *Gnomologia* (1732)

**Nothing is more
terrible than
ignorance in action.**

Johann Wolfgang von Goethe

Stupidity's the deliberate cultivation of ignorance.
WILLIAM GADDIS, in *Carpenter's Gothic* (1985)

You cannot know the intentions of a government
that doesn't know them itself.
JOHN KENNETH GALBRAITH, in *A Life in Our Times* (1981)

Noncooperation with evil is as much a duty
as is cooperation with good.
MOHANDAS GANDHI, statement in Indian court (Mar. 23, 1922)

Civility does not mean the mere outward
gentleness of speech cultivated for the occasion,
but an inborn gentleness and desire
to do the opponent good.
MOHANDAS GANDHI, quoted in S. Radhakrishnan,
Mahatma Gandhi (1939)

It is an indisputable fact that only vain people
wage war against the vanity of others.
MARGUERITE GARDINER (Lady Blessington), in
The Confessions of an Elderly Lady (1838)

We never injure our own characters so much
as when we attack those of others.
MARGUERITE GARDINER (Lady Blessington), in
Desultory Thoughts and Reflections (1839)

Lady Blessington was one of nineteenth century London's most prominent—and notorious—celebrities. After Lord Blessington, her husband of eleven years, died in 1829, she began a scandalous relationship with Count Alfred d'Orsay, the former husband of her stepdaughter.

The improbable couple went on to turn Gore House, their London home, into a salon that attracted the prominent writers and artists of the day. It was while serving as hostess of the salon that she wrote many popular books, including an 1834 book of conversations with Lord Byron and *Desultory Thoughts and Reflections,* a lovely little book of aphorisms about human fancies and foibles. In addition to the fore-going observation about a Trump specialty—attacking the character of others—the book contained these other relevant gems:

Mediocrity is only offensive
when accompanied by pretension.

There are no persons capable of stooping
so low as those who desire to rise in the world.

We are more prone to murmur at the
punishment of our faults than to lament them.

Experience has taught us little if it has not instructed
us to pity the errors of others, and to amend our own.

The vices of the rich and great are mistaken for errors,
and those of the poor and lowly for crimes.

Reason dissipates the illusions of life,
but does not console us for their departure.

Flattery, if judiciously administered, is always acceptable,
however much we may despise the flatterer.

Mountains appear more lofty,
the nearer they are approached,
but great men resemble them not in this particular.

Those who are formed to win general admiration,
are seldom calculated to bestow individual happiness.

When we find that we are not liked,
we assert that we are not understood;
when probably the dislike we have excited
proceeds from our being too fully comprehended.

Just because some people are liars...
is no reason why we should be fools.
ERLE STANLEY GARDNER, Perry Mason speaking, in
The Case of the Grinning Gorilla (1952)

Men of integrity, by their very existence,
rekindle the belief that as a people
we can live above the level of moral squalor.
We need that belief;
a cynical community is a corrupt community.
JOHN W. GARDNER, in *Excellence* (1961)

Gardner continued: "More than any other form of government democracy requires a certain optimism concerning mankind. The best argument for democracy is the existence of men who justify that optimism. It follows that one of the best ways to serve democracy is to be that kind of man."

The kind of service Gardner was urging requires *dedication*, about which he wrote: "Dedication is a condition of the highest reaches of performance. It is not possible to buy with money the highest levels of courage, faithfulness, or inspired performance."

How strange when an illusion dies
It's as though you've lost a child.

JUDY GARLAND, "An Illusion," in
Anne Edwards, *Judy Garland* (1975)

The winds and waves are always
on the side of the ablest navigators.

EDWARD GIBBON, in *Decline and Fall of the Roman Empire* (1788)

The nationalist has a broad hatred and a narrow love.

ANDRÉ GIDE, a 1918 journal entry

I owe much to my friends; but, all things considered,
it strikes me that I owe even more to my enemies.
The real person springs to life under a sting
even better than under a caress.

ANDRÉ GIDE, in *Pretexts: Reflections on Literature and Morality* (1959)

I can only say that politics, like misery,
"bring a man acquainted with strange bedfellows."

WILLIAM GIFFORD, in *The Baviad, and Maeviad* (1797)

This is the original expression of a sentiment that evolved into *politics makes strange bedfellows,* a saying that ultimately become so popular it completely supplanted the original Shakespeare passage that inspired it ("Misery acquaints a man with strange bedfellows," from *The Tempest*). The saying has been attributed to many others, but Gifford was the very first person to extend the concept from misery to politics.

I always voted at my party's call,
And I never thought of thinking for myself at all.

W. S. GILBERT, in *HMS Pinafore* (1878)

In every election in American history
both parties have their clichés.
The party that has the clichés that ring true wins.
NEWT GINGRICH, in the *International Herald Tribune* (Aug. 1, 1988)

A noble person attracts noble people,
and knows how to hold on to them.
JOHANN WOLFGANG VON GOETHE, in *Torquato Tasso* (1790)

None are more hopelessly enslaved
than those who falsely believe they are free.
JOHANN WOLFGANG VON GOETHE, in *Elective Affinities* (1808)

Nothing is more terrible than ignorance in action.
JOHANN WOLFGANG VON GOETHE, in *Proverbs in Prose* (1819)

One must *be* something in order to *do* something.
JOHANN WOLFGANG VON GOETHE, an 1828 remark, quoted
in J. P. Eckermann, *Conversations with Goethe* (1836)

Vanity is a desire of personal glory,
the wish to be appreciated, honored, and run after,
not because of one's personal qualities,
merits, and achievements, but
because of one's individual existence.
JOHANN WOLFGANG VON GOETHE, in *The Maxims
and Reflections of Goethe* (1906)

Never underestimate the insecurity of a star.
WILLIAM GOLDMAN, in *Adventures in the Screen Trade* (1983)

Silence gives consent.
OLIVER GOLDSMITH, in *The Good-Natur'd Man* (1768)

Feelings are self-justifying,
with a set of perceptions and "proofs" all their own.
DANIEL GOLEMAN, in *Emotional Intelligence* (1995)

His was the triumphant mien of the military commander
who has taken no active part in the
dust and heat of the battle, yet marches
very actively indeed at the head of his troops
when they return victoriously home.
ELIZABETH GOUDGE, in *The Little White Horse* (1946)

When people learn no tools of judgment
and merely follow their hopes,
the seeds of political manipulation are sown.
STEPHEN JAY GOULD, in *New York Review of Books* (Feb. 4, 1982)

In science, "fact" can only mean
"confirmed to such a degree that it would
be perverse to withhold provisional assent."
STEPHEN JAY GOULD, in *Hen's Teeth and Horse's Toes* (1983)

A single lie destroys a whole reputation for integrity.
BALTASAR GRACIÁN, in *The Art of Worldly Wisdom* (1647)

In 1995, nine out of ten evangelical Christians would have cited "a single lie" from Bill Clinton as compelling evidence of his lack of integrity. Now, twenty-five years later, and after more than 10,000 documented

Trump lies, what are we to make of this commitment to truth on behalf of so many members of the Religious Right?

The *Random House Dictionary* defines *integrity* this way: "Adherence to moral and ethical principles; soundness of moral character." The word itself derives from a Latin root meaning "whole; complete." The root sense, then, is that people are acting with integrity when their beliefs, words, and actions have a sense of unity or wholeness.

With people who lack integrity, there is a disconnect. They say things that are inconsistent with the truth or, worse, they say things they don't even believe. And when it comes to actions, it is a characteristic of integrity-challenged individuals that they frequently act in ways that run counter to their stated beliefs.

Exaggeration is a species of lying.
BALTASAR GRACIÁN, in *The Art of Worldly Wisdom* (1647)

Because the ignorant do not know themselves,
they never know for what they are lacking.
BALTASAR GRACIÁN, in *The Art of Worldly Wisdom* (1647)

Those who insist on the dignity of their office show they
have not deserved it, and that it is too much for them.
BALTASAR GRACIÁN, in *The Art of Worldly Wisdom* (1647)

Insecure people have a special sensitivity for anything
that finally confirms their own low opinion of themselves.
SUE GRAFTON, in *"B" is for Burglar* (1985)

Where ignorance is bliss,
'Tis folly to be wise.

THOMAS GRAY, in *Ode on a Distant
Prospect of Eton College* (1747)

There is such a thing as tempting the gods.
Talking too much, too soon, and with
too much self-satisfaction has always seemed
to me a sure way to court disaster.

MEG GREENFIELD, "The Rope and the Rack,"
Newsweek (Mar. 17, 1991)

Greenfield went on to add: "The forces of retribution are always listening. They never sleep."

There's nothing so dangerous for manipulators
as people who think for themselves.

MEG GREENFIELD, "The Last Word,"
in a 1988 issue of *Newsweek*

**Rudeness is
the weak man's
imitation of strength.**

Eric Hoffer

A very weak-minded fellow I am afraid,
and, like the feather pillow,
bears the marks of the last person who has sat on him!
DOUGLAS HAIG, on a contemporary politician; in
R. Blake, *Private Papers of Douglas Haig* (1952)

Haig originally offered this remarkable observation in 1918, and a strong case could be made that it also applies to Donald Trump. An April 2017 *Boston Globe* article titled, "Want to Change Trump's Mind on Policy? Be the Last One Who Talks to Him," was an early attempt to describe a phenomenon that's become even more familiar as his presidency has unfolded.

Success does not implant bad characteristics in people.
It merely steps up the growth rate
of the bad characteristics they already had.
MARGARET HALSEY, in *No Laughing Matter* (1977)

If...moral standards are conspicuously
and unprecedentedly breached in one area of society,
such as the political,
it will follow as the night the day that
those standards will start collapsing all down the line.
MARGARET HALSEY, in *No Laughing Matter* (1977)

Why has government been instituted at all?
Because the passions of men will not conform
to the dictates of reason and justice, without constraint.
ALEXANDER HAMILTON, in *The Federalist*
Papers, No. 15 (Dec. 1, 1787)

How often the great interests of society
are sacrificed to the vanity, to the conceit,
and to the obstinacy of individuals.

ALEXANDER HAMILTON, in *The Federalist
Papers, No. 70* (Mar. 18, 1788)

Hamilton went on to add: "Perhaps the question now before the public may…afford melancholy proofs of the effects of this despicable frailty, or rather detestable vice, in the human character."

No character, however upright, is a match
for constantly reiterated attacks, however false.

ALEXANDER HAMILTON, in *Observation on Certain Documents* (1797)

Hamilton was refuting charges made a year earlier that he had engaged in illegal speculation while serving as Secretary of the Treasury. He concluded by saying that an electorate who witness repeated attacks can easily become confused, and even suspicious of those who are falsely accused. They may, he suggested, be "apt in the end to sit down with the opinion that a person so often accused cannot be entirely innocent."

A nation which can prefer disgrace to danger
is prepared for a master, and deserves one.

ALEXANDER HAMILTON, in letter to *The Daily
Advertiser* (Feb. 21, 1797)

This much I think I do know—that a society so riven
that the spirit of moderation is gone, no court *can* save;
that in a society where that spirit
flourishes, no court *need* save.

LEARNED HAND, in speech in Boston, Mass. (Nov. 21, 1942)

The difference between patriotism and nationalism is that
the patriot is proud of his country for what it does,
and the nationalist is proud of his country
no matter what it does.

SYDNEY J. HARRIS, in *Strictly Personal* (1953)

There is no delusion more fatal, no folly more profound,
than a man's belief that he can kick and
gouge and scheme his way to the top—
and then afford the luxury of being a good person;
for no consequence is more certain than
that we *become* what we *do.*

SYDNEY J. HARRIS, in *Last Things First* (1961)

There are moral imbeciles just as there are mental imbeciles;
but while the latter are recognized
as having an inborn defect
and are put away where they can do no harm,
the former often acquire great power in the world—
yet the man born with a deficient moral sense
is a thousand times more dangerous
than the mental defective.

SYDNEY J. HARRIS, in *Last Things First* (1961)

A person who has no genuine sense of pity
for the weak is missing a basic source of strength,
for one of the prime moral forces that
comprise greatness and strength of character
is a feeling of mercy

SYDNEY J. HARRIS, in *On the Contrary* (1964)

Harris added: "The ruthless man…is always a weak and frightened man."

**What the essential difference between the wise man
and the ignorant man boils down to is this:
the wise man will often know without judging,
while the ignorant man will judge without knowing.**
SYDNEY J. HARRIS, in *Leaving the Surface* (1968)

**Goethe was wrong;
there is one thing more terrible than
imagination without taste,
and that is power without intelligence.**
SYDNEY J. HARRIS, in *For the Time Being* (1972)

Harris was piggybacking on a popular observation from Johann Wolfgang von Goethe: "There is nothing more dreadful than imagination without taste."

**The difference between a good person and a bad person
(and each of us is a little of both, naturally)
is really very simple at bottom:
The good person loves people and uses things,
while the bad person loves things and uses people.**
SYDNEY J. HARRIS, in *Pieces of Eight* (1982)

"Elitism" is the slur directed at merit by mediocrity.
SYDNEY J. HARRIS, in *Pieces of Eight* (1982)

Truth—which is the first casualty of tyranny.
BARBARA GRIZZUTI HARRISON, tweaking the popular
saying, in *The Astonishing World* (1992)

Bragging is not merely designed to impress.
Bragging is designed to produce envy and assert superiority.
It is, therefore, an act of hostility.
AARON HASS, in Doing the Right Thing (1998)

Hass continued: "Bragging is also a transparent ploy. It reveals your lack of self-confidence. 'I am not enough,' you feel. So you resort to showering me with your 'achievements' in order to mask your perceived deficiencies."

It is to the credit of human nature that,
except where its selfishness is brought into play,
it loves more readily than it hates.
NATHANIEL HAWTHORNE, in The Scarlet Letter (1850)

The words come from the novel's narrator, who continues with a thought that captures what Donald Trump has attempted to do with his base for the past several years: "Hatred, by a gradual and quiet process, will even be transformed into love *unless* [italics mine] the change be impeded by a continually new irritation of the original feeling of hostility."

No man, for any considerable period,
can wear one face to himself and another to the multitude,
without finally getting bewildered as
to which may be the true.
NATHANIEL HAWTHORNE, in The Scarlet Letter (1850)

Nothing can be more true than that
the greatest Boasters have the least of what they pretend to.
ELIZA HAYWOOD, in Love-Letters on All Occasions (1730)

Those who are unjust in one thing,
will be so in others.

ELIZA HAYWOOD, in *Love-Letters on All Occasions* (1730)

Envy is a littleness of soul,
which cannot see beyond a certain point,
and if it does not occupy the whole space,
feels itself excluded.

WILLIAM HAZLITT, in *Characteristics* (1823)

There are names written in her immortal
scroll at which Fame blushes!

WILLIAM HAZLITT, in *Characteristics* (1823)

If no thought
your mind does visit,
make your speech
not too explicit.

PIET HEIN, "The Case for Obscurity," in *Grooks* (1966)

Man is not a rational animal;
he is a rationalizing animal.

ROBERT A. HEINLEIN, "Gulf," in *Astounding
Science Fiction* (Oct.-Nov. 1949)

It is a truism that almost any sect, cult, or religion
will legislate its creed into law
if it acquires the political power to do so.

ROBERT A. HEINLEIN, in *Revolt in 2100* (1953)

Heinlein went on to add: "This is equally true whether the faith is Communism or Holy-Rollerism; indeed it is the bounden duty of the faithful to do so. The custodians of the True Faith cannot logically admit tolerance of heresy to be a virtue."

A *dying* culture invariably exhibits personal rudeness.
Bad manners. Lack of consideration
for others in minor matters.
A loss of politeness, of gentle manners,
is more significant than is a riot.

ROBERT A. HEINLEIN, in *Friday* (1982)

You know, that might be the answer—
to act boastfully about something we
ought to be ashamed of.
That's a trick that never seems to fail.

JOSEPH HELLER, in *Catch-22* (1961)

Even among men lacking all distinction
he inevitably stood out as a man lacking more distinction
than all the rest, and people who met him
were always impressed by how unimpressive he was.

JOSEPH HELLER, in *Catch-22* (1961)

This was the narrator's description of Major Major in Heller's classic novel. He preceded the observation with another classic line, a tweak of one of Shakespeare's most famous passages: "Some men are born mediocre, some men achieve mediocrity, and some have mediocrity thrust upon them."

It is an error to suppose that no man
understands his own character.
Most persons know even their failings very well,
only they persist in giving them names different from
those usually assigned by the rest of the world; and they
compensate for this mistake by naming, at first sight,
with singular accuracy, those very same failings in others.

ARTHUR HELPS, in *Thoughts in the Cloister and the Crowd* (1835)

To keep your character intact
you cannot stoop to filthy acts.
It makes it easier to stoop the next time.

KATHARINE HEPBURN, quoted in *The Los
Angeles Times* (Nov. 24, 1974)

A man's character is his fate.

HERACLITUS, in *On the Universe* (6th c. BC)

When religion and politics travel in the same cart,
the riders believe nothing can stand in their way.

FRANK HERBERT, in *Dune* (1965)

When a wise man does not understand, he says:
"I do not understand."
The fool and the uncultured are ashamed of their ignorance.
They remain silent when a question
could bring them wisdom.

FRANK HERBERT, in *The Godmakers* (1972)

Don't give over all of your critical
faculties to people in power,
no matter how admirable those people may appear to be.
FRANK HERBERT, "Dune Genesis," in *Omni* (July 1980)

Herbert continued: "Beneath the hero's facade you will find a human being who makes human mistakes. Enormous problems arise when human mistakes are made on the grand scale available to a superhero."

The people I distrust most are those
who want to improve our lives
but have only one course of action in mind.
FRANK HERBERT, "The Plowboy Interview," in
Mother Earth News (May/June 1981)

All governments suffer a recurring problem:
Power attracts pathological personalities.
It is not that power corrupts
but that it is magnetic to the corruptible.
FRANK HERBERT, in *Chapterhouse: Dune* (1985)

My view of history says mistakes made by a leader
(or made in a leader's name) are amplified by
the numbers who follow without question.
FRANK HERBERT, in Introduction to *Eye* (1987)

I've noticed that ineffectual people
usually do go in for highfalutin' threats.
GEORGETTE HEYER, in *The Unfinished Clue* (1937)

I have learned by experience that no man's character
can be eventually injured but by his own acts.
ROWLAND HILL, in E. Sidney, The Life of Rev. Rowland Hill (1833)

Religious ideas, supposedly private matters
between man and god, are in practice always political ideas.
CHRISTOPHER HITCHENS, in The Monarchy (1990)

We lie loudest when we lie to ourselves.
ERIC HOFFER, in The Passionate State of Mind (1955)

Rudeness is the weak man's imitation of strength.
ERIC HOFFER, in The Passionate State of Mind (1955)

The hardest thing to cope with
is not selfishness or vanity or deceitfulness,
but sheer stupidity.
ERIC HOFFER, in The Passionate State of Mind (1955)

The only index by which to judge a
government or a way of life
is by the quality of the people it acts upon.
No matter how noble the objectives of a government,
if it blurs decency and kindness, cheapens human life,
and breeds ill will and suspicion—it is an evil government.
ERIC HOFFER, in The Passionate State of Mind (1955)

I detest the man who hides one thing
in the depths of his heart, and speaks forth another.
HOMER, Achilles speaking, in Iliad (8th c. BC)

When there is a lack of honor in government,
the morals of the whole people are poisoned.
HERBERT HOOVER, in *The New York Times* (Aug. 9, 1964)

People never have confidence in a Big Talker.
They know his statements must be cut down,
but they can never tell how much.
EDGAR WATSON HOWE, in *Country Town Sayings* (1911)

The only foes that threaten America
are the enemies at home, and these are
ignorance, superstition, and incompetence.
ELBERT HUBBARD, in *The Philistine* (Jan. 1905)

The recipe for perpetual ignorance is:
Be satisfied with your opinions
and content with your knowledge.
ELBERT HUBBARD, in *The Philistine* (May 1907)

When you cannot reply to a man's arguments
all is not lost— you can still call him vile names.
ELBERT HUBBARD, "East of Suez," in *The Philistine* (Dec. 1914)

Strong men can always afford to be gentle.
Only the weak are intent on "giving as good as they get."
ELBERT HUBBARD, in *The Note Book* (1927)

Nothing appears more surprising to those,
who consider human affairs with a philosophical eye,
than the easiness with which the many
are governed by the few;
and the implicit submission, with which men resign
their own sentiments and passions to those of their rulers.

DAVID HUME, "Of the First Principles of
Government," in *Essays* (1741-1742)

Where men are the most sure and arrogant,
they are commonly the most mistaken,
and have there given reins to passion,
without that proper deliberation and suspense,
which can alone secure them from the grossest absurdities.

DAVID HUME, in *An Enquiry Concerning the
Principles of Morals* (1751)

The corruption of the best things gives rise to the worst.

DAVID HUME, in *The Natural History of Religion* (1757)

The death of democracy is not likely to be
an assassination from ambush.
It will be a slow extinction from
apathy, indifference, and undernourishment.

ROBERT M. HUTCHINS, in *Great Books* (1954)

The pleasures of ignorance are as great,
in their way, as the pleasures of knowledge.

ALDOUS HUXLEY, "Meditation on El Greco," in *Music at Night* (1931)

Most ignorance is vincible ignorance.
We don't know because we don't want to know.
It is our will which decides how
and upon what subjects we shall use our intelligence.
ALDOUS HUXLEY, in *Ends and Means* (1938)

Reality cannot be ignored except at a price;
and the longer the ignorance is persisted in,
the higher and the more terrible
becomes the price that must be paid.
ALDOUS HUXLEY, in *Vedanta for the Western World* (1945)

An unexciting truth may be eclipsed
by a thrilling falsehood.
ALDOUS HUXLEY, in *Brave New World Revisited* (1958)

Assembled in a crowd, people lose their
powers of reasoning and their capacity for moral choice.
ALDOUS HUXLEY, in *Brave New World Revisited* (1958)

At this point we find ourselves
confronted by a very disquieting question:
Do we really wish to act upon our knowledge?
ALDOUS HUXLEY, in *Brave New World Revisited* (1958)

There is no sea more dangerous than
the ocean of practical politics—
none in which there is more need of good pilotage
and of a single, unfaltering purpose
when the waves rise high.
T. H. HUXLEY, in "On the Natural Inequality of Men" (1890)

I

Only the
very ignorant are
perfectly satisfied
that they know.

Robert G. Ingersoll

Look into any man's heart you please,
and you will always find, in every one,
at least one black spot which he has to keep concealed.
HENRIK IBSEN, in Pillars of Society (1877)

Castles in the air—they're so easy to take refuge in.
So easy to build, too.
HENRIK IBSEN, in The Master Builder (1892)

Who make up the majority in any given country?
Is it the wise men or the fools?
I think we must agree that the fools are in a terrible,
overwhelming majority, all the world over.
HENRIK IBSEN, in An Enemy of the People (1882)

The question is posed—and answered—by the character Dr. Stock-mann. He continues: "But how in the devil's name can it ever be right for fools to rule over wise men?"

Arguments cannot be answered with insults.
ROBERT G. INGERSOLL, "The Christian Religion," in
The North American Review (Nov. 1881)

Epithets are the arguments of malice.
ROBERT G. INGERSOLL, "The Christian Religion," in
The North American Review (Nov. 1881)

Only the very ignorant
are perfectly satisfied that they know.
ROBERT G. INGERSOLL, in Liberty in Literature (1890)

Nothing discloses real character like the use of power.
ROBERT G. INGERSOLL, in A. T. Rice, *Reminiscences
of Abraham Lincoln* (1885)

This observation is almost always mistakenly attributed to Abraham Lincoln, but Ingersoll is the author. He continued by writing: "It is easy for the weak to be gentle. Most people can bear adversity. But if you wish to know what a man really is, give him power. This is the supreme test."

Ingersoll, one of the leading orators of the era and a powerful figure in the Republican Party, originally offered his words in an 1885 tribute to the sixteenth president. He concluded his piece by writing: "It is the glory of Lincoln that, having almost absolute power, he never abused it, except upon the side of mercy."

**A tart temper never mellows with age,
and a sharp tongue is the only edged tool
that grows keener with constant use.**
WASHINGTON IRVING, in "Rip Van Winkle" (1820)

**Nice is a pallid virtue.
Not like honesty or courage or perseverance.
On the other hand, in a nation frequently lacking in civility,
there is much to be said for nice.**
MOLLY IVINS, in *Fort Worth Star-Telegram* (May 15, 1994)

**When politicians start talking about
large groups of their fellow Americans as "enemies,"
it's time for a quiet stir of alertness.
Polarizing people is a good way to win an election,
and also a good way to wreck a country.**
MOLLY IVINS, in *You Got to Dance with Them What Brung You* (1998)

Gratitude is a fruit
of great cultivation;
you do not find it
among gross people.

Samuel Johnson

If there is any fixed star in our constitutional constellation,
it is that no official, high or petty,
can prescribe what shall be orthodox in politics,
nationalism, religion, or other matters of opinion
or force citizens to confess by word
or action their faith within.

ROBERT H. JACKSON, in *W. Virginia State
Bd. of Educ. V. Barnette* (1943)

Men are more often bribed
by their loyalties and ambitions than money.

ROBERT H. JACKSON, in *United States v. Wunderlich* (1951)

Perfect love may cast out fear,
but fear is remarkably potent in casting out love.

P. D. JAMES, tweaking 1 John 4:18, in *Time to Be in Earnest* (1999)

The hell to be endured hereafter, of which theology tells,
is no worse than the hell we make
for ourselves in this world by habitually
fashioning our characters in the wrong way.

WILLIAM JAMES, in *Talks to Teachers on Psychology* (1899)

We are all ready to be savage in *some* cause.
The difference between a good man and a bad one
is the choice of the cause.

WILLIAM JAMES, in letter to E. L. Godkin (Dec. 24, 1895)

He who permits himself to tell a lie once
finds it much easier to do it a second and third time,
till at length it becomes habitual;
he tells lies without attending to it,
and truths without the world's believing him.

THOMAS JEFFERSON, in letter to nephew Peter Carr (Aug. 19, 1785)

Jefferson continued: "This falsehood of the tongue leads to that of the heart, and in time depraves all its good dispositions."

What is it that men cannot be made to believe!

THOMAS JEFFERSON, in letter to Richard Henry Lee (Apr. 22, 1786)

I find the pain of a little censure,
even when it is unfounded,
is more acute than the pleasure of much praise.

THOMAS JEFFERSON, in letter to Francis Hopkinson (Mar. 13, 1789)

I am sure that in estimating
every man's value either in private or public life,
a pure integrity is the quality we take first into calculation,
and that learning and talents are only the second.

THOMAS JEFFERSON, in letter to John Garland
Jefferson (June 15, 1792)

I never saw an instance of one of two disputants
convincing the other by argument.

THOMAS JEFFERSON, in letter to John Taylor (June 1, 1798)

When a man assumes a public trust,
he should consider himself as public property.

THOMAS JEFFERSON, in 1807 letter to Baron Wilhelm von Humboldt

He who knows most, knows how little he knows.
THOMAS JEFFERSON, in "Batture at New Orleans" (1812)

It is in our lives, and not from our words,
that our religion must be read.
THOMAS JEFFERSON, in letter to Mrs. Samuel H. Smith (Aug. 6, 1816)

You can get so anesthetized by your
own pain or your own problem
that you don't quite fully share the
hell of someone close to you.
LADY BIRD JOHNSON, in *White House Diary* (1970)

A generous and elevated mind is distinguished by
nothing more certainly than an eminent degree of curiosity.
SAMUEL JOHNSON, a 1735 remark, quoted in James
Boswell, *Life of Samuel Johnson* (1791)

Dr. Johnson—who exhibited a deep and vibrant curiosity his entire life—also appreciated the trait in others. He reprised the sentiment above sixteen years later in an essay in *The Rambler* (March 12, 1751), writing: "Curiosity is one of the permanent and certain characteristics of a vigorous intellect."

Outside of a handful of sycophants, few people would describe Donald Trump as having an elevated curiosity or a vigorous intellect. Indeed, the people who've followed him for decades are virtually unanimous in describing him as a remarkably incurious man who prefers television viewing over the reading of any printed material (unless, of course, that printed material contains something positive about him).

As Trump was seeking the Republican nomination, this long-standing trait was frequently discussed, but never better than in an April 2016 syndicated column ("Trump's Fatal Flaw: Lack of Curiosity") by political satirist Mark Shields. Struck by the presidential candidate's stunning lack of knowledge, Shields wrote: "The front-runner Donald Trump has a fatal flaw: He is a man who has been unchallenged by flatterers and sycophants for so long, that by now he is almost terminally uncurious." Clearly, Shield's article didn't resonate with the mass of Republican voters, but it certainly impressed those of us who love a clever turn of phrase, for he ended it this way: "American voters will now ask the arrogantly uncurious Trump a simple question: If you're so rich, why aren't you smart?"

**When once the forms of civility are violated,
there remains little hope of return to kindness or decency.**
SAMUEL JOHNSON, in *The Rambler* (Sep. 25, 1750)

**Almost all absurdity of conduct arises from
the imitation of those whom we cannot resemble.**
SAMUEL JOHNSON, in *The Rambler* (July 2, 1751)

**No estimate is more in danger of erroneous calculation
than those by which a man computes
the force of his own genius.**
SAMUEL JOHNSON, in *The Rambler* (Sep. 7, 1751)

**Ignorance, when it is voluntary, is criminal.
And he may properly be charged with evil,
who refused to learn how he might prevent it.**
SAMUEL JOHNSON, in *The History of Rasselas* (1759)

**Gratitude is a fruit of great cultivation;
you do not find it among gross people.**
SAMUEL JOHNSON, a 1773 remark, quoted in J. Boswell,
Journal of a Tour to the Hebrides (1785)

Patriotism is the last refuge of a scoundrel.
SAMUEL JOHNSON, a 1775 remark, quoted in James
Boswell, *Life of Samuel Johnson* (1791)

This is one of quotation history's most celebrated observations, and this is the way it's almost always presented. Boswell took pains, however, to clarify that Johnson was talking about "pretended patriotism" and not the real thing. Here's his original entry:

> "Patriotism having become one of our topics, Johnson suddenly uttered, in a strong determined tone, an apothegm at which many will start: 'Patriotism is the last refuge of a scoundrel.' But let it be considered, that he did not mean a real and generous love of our country, but that pretended patriotism which so many, in all ages and countries, have made a cloak of self-interest."

Over the years, Johnson's famous observation has inspired numerous tweaks and spin-offs. One of the best appeared in the "patriotism" entry of *The Devil's Dictionary* (1911), where Ambrose Bierce wrote:

> "In Dr. Johnson's famous dictionary, patriotism is defined as the last resort of a scoundrel. With all due respect to an enlightened but inferior lexicographer I beg to submit that it is the first."

It is more from carelessness about truth
than from intentional lying that there is
so much falsehood in the world.

SAMUEL JOHNSON, a March 31, 1778 remark, quoted in
James Boswell, *Life of Samuel Johnson* (1791)

The insolence of wealth will creep out.

SAMUEL JOHNSON, an April 18, 1778 remark, quoted in
James Boswell, *Life of Samuel Johnson* (1791)

One of the great secrets of the day is to know how
to take possession of popular prejudices and passions,
in such a way as to introduce a confusion of principles
which makes impossible all understanding between those
who speak the same language and have the same interests.

MAURICE JOLY, the character Niccolo Machiavelli speaking, in *The
Dialogue in Hell Between Machiavelli and Montesquieu* (1864)

Joly's book, which uses the popular literary device of a dialogue between the dead, was an attack on the reign of Napoleon III. When the two historical figures meet in hell, a debate on politics ensues, with Machiavelli representing the forces of despotism and Montesquieu making the case for liberal democracies. When I first came across this quotation in my research, I was particularly struck by how it captured a signature Trump strategy: attempting to confuse people about guiding principles by *taking possession of popular prejudices and passions.*

Beware of the man who wants to protect you;
he will protect you from everything but himself.

ERICA JONG, in *Half-Lives* (1971)

> The stakes are too high for government
> to be a spectator sport.
> BARBARA C. JORDAN, in 1977 speech at Harvard University

A decade later, Marian Wright Edelman expressed the idea more succinctly in *Families in Peril* (1987): "Democracy is not a spectator sport."

> Mediocrity is excellence to the mediocre.
> JOSEPH JOUBERT, in *Pensées* (1842)

> A part of kindness consists in
> loving people more than they deserve.
> JOSEPH JOUBERT, in *Pensées* (1842)

> Those who never retract their opinions
> love themselves more than they love truth.
> JOSEPH JOUBERT, in *Pensées* (1842)

> Mistakes are, after all, the foundations of truth,
> and if a man does not know what a thing *is*, it is at least
> an increase in knowledge if he knows what it is *not*.
> CARL JUNG, "The Structure and Dynamics of the Self," in *Aion* (1951)

Mistakes are the foundations of truth only when people admit to making them, and this is not exactly a Trump specialty. To say that our forty-fifth president has difficulty acknowledging a mistake is a vast understatement, for he's taken this trait to what most people would regard as extreme lengths. Countless examples could be cited, but let me mention only one. At a 2019 White House roundtable meeting of business leaders, Trump inadvertently referred to Tim Cook, the CEO of Apple, as "Tim Apple." It was a "human" moment that was widely broadcast in news programs later in the day.

This innocent slip of the tongue was the kind of mistake all of us have made, and Trump could have endeared himself to millions if he had simply made a self-effacing remark about it. But it is a hallmark of insecure people that they cannot admit to a mistake. A few days later, Trump told a group of Republican donors that he said, "Tim Cook, Apple," but he said it so fast people didn't hear his exact words. When that claim was proven false, Trump further revised his story in a March 11, 2019 tweet:

> "At a recent round table meeting of business executives, & long after formally introducing Tim Cook of Apple, I quickly referred to Tim + Apple as Tim/Apple as an easy way to save time & words. The Fake News was disparagingly all over this, & it became yet another bad Trump story!"

The wise man who is not heeded is counted a fool,
and the fool who proclaims the general folly
first and loudest passes for a prophet.
CARL JUNG, in *Mysterium Coniunctionis* (1955)

If one does not understand a person,
one tends to regard him as a fool.
CARL JUNG, in *Mysterium Coniunctionis* (1955)

It is sometimes difficult to avoid the impression
that there is a sort of foreknowledge of
the coming series of events.
CARL JUNG, in *Synchronicity* (1960)

Revenge is always the pleasure of a paltry, feeble, tiny mind.
JUVENAL, in *Satires* (2nd c. AD)

> **Nature, in giving tears to man, confessed that he**
> **had a tender heart; this is our noblest quality.**
>
> JUVENAL, in *Satires* (2nd c. AD)

We've all occasionally seen an American president moistening up with a tear or trying to maintain composure during a deeply emotionally moment. It doesn't happen very often, but when it does, we're witnessing what Juvenal would say is a leader's "noblest quality." That we've never seen a moment like this with President Trump is telling, and brings to mind one additional thought on the subject. In *Elective Affinities* (1808), Johann Wolfgang von Goethe wrote: "Men who give way easily to tears are good. I have nothing to do with those whose hearts are dry and whose eyes are dry!"

**It's only because
of their stupidity
that they're able to be
so sure of themselves.**

Franz Kafka

They're talking about things of which
they don't have the slightest understanding, anyway.
It's only because of their stupidity
that they're able to be so sure of themselves.
FRANZ KAFKA, in *The Trial* (1920)

What makes fantastic declarations believable...
is, in part, the vehemence with which they're proffered...
intensity of personal belief is evidence of truth.
WENDY KAMINER, in *Sleeping with Extra-Terrestrials* (1999)

Here, Kaminer was specifically referring to the world of celebrity, spirituality, and pop psychology, but I'm sure she'd be comfortable with her contention being extended to the many fantastic declarations Donald Trump has made over the years.

By a lie a human being throws away and,
as it were, annihilates his dignity as a human being.
IMMANUEL KANT, in *The Metaphysics of Morals* (1797)

Arrogance is, as it were,
a solicitation on the part of one seeking honor
for followers, whom he thinks he is
entitled to treat with contempt.
IMMANUEL KANT, in *The Metaphysics of Morals* (1797)

Kant went on to write that arrogant, self-serving people also often attempt to smear and badmouth others. About these practices, he wrote: "It is, therefore, a duty of virtue not to take malicious pleasure in exposing the faults of others so that one will be thought of as good as, or at least not worse than, others."

I distrust the rash optimism in this country that cries,
"Hurrah, we're all right!
This is the greatest nation on earth,"
when there are grievances that call loudly for redress.
HELEN KELLER, in *Optimism* (1903)

Science may have found a cure for most evils;
but it has found no remedy for the worst of them all—
the apathy of human beings.
HELEN KELLER, in *My Religion* (1927)

Once you know something is wrong, you're responsible,
whether you see it, or hear about it,
and most particularly when you're a part of it.
M. E. KERR (pen name of Marijane Meaker), in *Gentlehands* (1978)

Using insult instead of argument is the sign of a small mind.
LAURIE R. KING, the character Sherlock Holmes
speaking, in *O Jerusalem* (1999)

Nothing in all the world is more dangerous
than sincere ignorance and conscientious stupidity.
MARTIN LUTHER KING, Jr., in *Strength to Love* (1963)

Returning hate for hate multiplies hate,
adding deeper darkness to a night already devoid of stars.
Darkness cannot drive out darkness;
only light can do that.
MARTIN LUTHER KING, Jr., in *Strength to Love* (1963)

A meaningless phrase repeated again and again
begins to resemble truth.
BARBARA KINGSOLVER, in *Animal Dreams* (1990)

Words matter. Words can destroy.
What we call each other ultimately becomes
what we think of each other, and it matters.
JEANE J. KIRKPATRICK, in 1982 Anti-Defamation League address

The highly ambitious person, in spite of
all his successes, always remains dissatisfied,
in the same way as a greedy baby is never satisfied.
MELANIE KLEIN, in "Our Adult World and Its Roots in Infancy" (1959)

Words can be like tiny doses of arsenic:
they are swallowed unnoticed, appear to have no effect,
and then after a little time the toxic reaction sets in after all.
VICTOR KLEMPERER, in *The Language of the Third Reich* (1946; 2000)

Klemperer preceded the observation by writing: "What happens if the
cultivated language is made up of poisonous elements or has been
made the bearer of poisons?"

Klemperer's book, originally published in German in 1946, was a language expert's analysis of the rise of Nazism in Germany. He began
the discussion with this intriguing observation about how the Nazis
came to exert such control over German citizens:

"The most powerful influence was exerted neither by individual speeches nor by articles or flyers, posters or flags;
it was not achieved by things which one had to absorb by
conscious thought or conscious emotions. Instead Nazism
permeated the flesh and blood of the people through

single words, idioms, and sentence structures which were imposed on them in a million repetitions and taken on board mechanically and unconsciously."

Every two years the American politics industry fills the airwaves with the most virulent, scurrilous, wall-to-wall character assassination of nearly every political practitioner in the country—and then declares itself puzzled that America has lost trust in its politicians.

CHARLES KRAUTHAMMER, "Political Suicide," in
The Washington Post (Oct. 28, 1994)

**Eminent posts make
great men greater,
and little men less.**

Jean de La Bruyère

Profound ignorance makes a man dogmatic.
JEAN DE LA BRUYÈRE, in *The Characters* (1688)

The man who knows nothing thinks he is
teaching others what he has just learned himself.
JEAN DE LA BRUYÈRE, in *The Characters* (1688)

When Trump says, "Nobody knows," "People don't realize," "A lot of people don't know," or similar expressions, it has become an inside joke among journalists that he always means the same thing: "I had no clue about this until somebody filled me in recently." Eli Stokel, a *Washington Post* journalist, described the frequent use of such phrases as "Trump's tells." When Trump says such things, Stokel suggests, it should be interpreted as: "That's code for I just found this out."

Eminent posts make great men greater,
and little men less.
JEAN DE LA BRUYÈRE, in *The Characters* (1688)

True greatness is free, kind, familiar and popular;
it lets itself be touched and handled,
it loses nothing by being seen at close quarters;
the better one knows it, the more one admires it.
JEAN DE LA BRUYÈRE, in *The Characters* (1688)

La Bruyère was contrasting true greatness with false greatness, which he described this way: "It hides…and reveals itself only enough to create an illusion and not be recognized as the meanness that it really is."

Incivility is not a vice of the soul,
but the effect of several vices;
of vanity, ignorance of duty, laziness, stupidity,
distraction, contempt of others, and jealousy.

JEAN DE LA BRUYÈRE, in *The Characters* (1688)

When once a social order is well established,
no matter what injustice it involves,
those who occupy a position of advantage
are not long in coming to believe that
it is the only possible and reasonable order.

SUZANNE LA FOLLETTE, in *Concerning Women* (1926)

It is the common failing of an
ambitious mind to over-rate itself.

CAROLINE LAMB, in *Glenaryon* (1816)

No man has the right to be ignorant.
In a country like this, ignorance is a crime.

LOUIS L'AMOUR, in *Sackett: A Novel* (1961)

The words come from protagonist Tell Sackett, who continues: "If a man is going to vote, if he's going to take part in his country and his government, then it's up to him to understand."

There is no greater role for a man to play
than to assist in the government of a people,
nor anyone lower than he who misuses that power.

LOUIS L'AMOUR, in *The Lonesome Gods* (1983)

This reflection from protagonist and narrator Johannes Verne was complemented later in the novel by a related thought: "If men are to survive upon the earth there must be law, and there must be justice, and all men must stand together against those who would strike at the roots of what men have so carefully built."

Honor can be a troublesome thing,
but if one has it one does not lightly yield it.

LOUIS L'AMOUR, in *The Walking Drum* (1984)

Years from now, the question for many who functioned in and around the Trump presidency will be, "Did I act with honor?" Of course, most of those who yielded their honor to expediency and party loyalty will find a way to rationalize their choices, but they will likely have children and grandchildren who arrive at a different conclusion.

I have reverence for truth, but I do not know what truth is.
I suspect that there are many truths, and therefore,
I suspect all who claim to have *the* truth.

LOUIS L'AMOUR, in *The Walking Drum* (1984)

His primary rules were:
never allow the public to cool off;
never admit a fault or wrong; never concede
that there may be some good in your enemy;
never leave room for alternatives;
never accept blame;
concentrate on one enemy at a time and
blame him for everything that goes wrong;
people will believe a big lie sooner than a little one;
and if you repeat it frequently enough
people will sooner or later believe it.

W. C. LANGER, a 1943 profile of Hitler, in *The Mind of*
Adolf Hitler: The Secret Wartime Report (1973)

Walter Langer was the principal author of "A Psychological Analysis of Adolph Hitler," a secret 1943 report commissioned by the United States Office of Strategic Services. A few years earlier, Langer, a successful Boston psychoanalyst had begun talking with William "Wild Bill" Donovan, head of the O.S.S., about psychological warfare. During one of those conversations, Donovan asked Langer if he could write something in plain English that would help to explain "What makes Hitler tick."

Self-love is the greatest of all flatterers.
FRANÇOIS, Duc de La Rochefoucauld, in *Maximes* (1665)

Brought up in one of France's most aristocratic families, La Rochefoucauld received the education one would expect of a young gentleman-in-training. In addition to private tutoring in Latin, Greek, history, mathematics, and philosophy, he learned how to fence, hunt, dance, and behave properly in the king's court. While still in his teens, he also became a decorated veteran of French battles in Italy and other European countries. By early adulthood, he was the model of a sophisticated French nobleman.

At age forty, he was stripped of his titles after his involvement with the Fronde (a group of disaffected French aristocrats) failed to overthrow the monarchy. Ousted from the family estate, he was badly wounded and without much hope when, during his recovery, he began re-reading the Greek and Roman classics he first studied in his youth. Viewing them from a more mature perspective, he began recording his personal thoughts and reflections. In 1665, he published *Maximes,* a volume of about 500 observations stimulated by his reading of ancient authors.

As the years passed, La Rochefoucauld continued to unveil more of his creations in subsequent editions. *Maximes* went on to become one of history's great literary treasures (in continuous print for more than 350 years) and La Rochefoucauld is often hailed as "history's greatest aphorist." As with the *self-love* quotation above, many of his observations attempted to expose the hypocrisy, pretentiousness, and self-deception he observed—especially in the upper classes of French society. Not surprisingly, many of his sayings bring aspects of Trump's functioning to mind:

Small minds are hurt by the smallest things

> The truest way to be deceived is to
> think oneself more knowing than others.

We try to make virtues out of
the faults we have no wish to correct.

> The world more often rewards the
> appearance of merit than merit itself.

If vanity does not overthrow all virtues,
at least she makes them totter.

> It is the habit of mediocre minds to
> condemn all that is beyond their grasp.

If we had no faults of our own, we should not
take so much pleasure in noticing those in others.

> Flattery is counterfeit money which,
> but for vanity, would have no circulation.

The qualities we have do not make us
so ridiculous as those which we affect to have.

> The most violent passions sometimes leave us
> at rest, but vanity agitates us constantly.

It is as easy to deceive ourselves without noticing
as it is hard to deceive others without their noticing.

> We are eager to believe that others are flawed
> because we are eager to believe in what we wish for.

Our enemies come nearer the truth in the opinions they
form of us than we do in our opinion of ourselves.

The man who thinks he can
do without the world is indeed mistaken;
the man who thinks the world cannot
do without him is mistaken even worse.

The stamp of great minds
is to suggest much in few words;
by contrast, little minds have the gift
of talking a great deal and saying nothing.

Office tends to confer a dreadful plausibility
on even the most negligible of those who hold it.
MARK LAWSON, in Introduction to Joe
Queenan's *Imperial Caddy* (1992)

Lawson was writing about yet another politician who seemed too small for the position he held—vice president Dan Quayle during the first Bush administration—and his point remains true today: simply occupying an important government position lends a certain legitimacy even to those who lack the qualifications for the office.

Egotism is the anesthetic that dulls the pain of stupidity.
FRANK LEAHY, in *Look* (Jan. 10, 1955)

The only fool bigger than the person who knows it all
is the person who argues with him
STANISLAW JERZY LEC, in *Unkempt Thoughts* (1957)

Stanislaw Jerzy Lec, an aspiring writer of Jewish-Ukrainian heritage, was serving in the Polish army in 1941 when he was captured by German troops and interred in a work camp. Two years later, after killing a Nazi guard with a shovel he'd been given to dig his own grave, he made a daring escape in which he avoided detection by dressing in the guard's uniform. After the war, he resumed his pre-war writing career and became a familiar name in Eastern Europe.

Lec was virtually unknown in the west when, in 1962, St. Martin's Press published an English version of *Unkempt Thoughts*, a collection of his aphorisms. Almost immediately, he was hailed by critics as a major satirist and a brilliant aphorist. A sequel, *More Unkempt Thoughts*, appeared in 1969, and both books have made Lec a legend among quotation lovers worldwide. Many of his creations, as in the foregoing observation about arguing with a know-it-all, are perfectly relevant in any discussion of Trump and his vocal Trumpeteers:

Even his ignorance is encyclopedic.

When reasons are weak, attitudes stiffen.

Sometimes you have to be silent to be heard.

Every scarecrow has a secret ambition to terrorize.

No snowflake in an avalanche ever feels responsible.

Impartiality is not neutrality—it is partiality for justice.

Every stink that fights the ventilator thinks it is Don Quixote.

**The weakest link in the chain is also the strongest.
It can break the chain.**

**The face of the enemy frightens me only
when I see how much it resembles mine.**

Thoughts, like fleas, jump from man to man.
But they don't bite everybody.

It's never an insult to be called
what somebody thinks is a bad name.
It just shows you how poor that person is,
it doesn't hurt you.
HARPER LEE, in *To Kill a Mockingbird* (1960)

You never really understand a person
until you consider things from his point of view—
until you climb into his skin and walk around in it.
HARPER LEE, in *To Kill a Mockingbird* (1960)

Darkness is only in the mortal eye,
that thinks it sees, but sees not.
URSULA K. LE GUIN, in *The Left Hand of Darkness* (1969)

You cannot blame everything on the enemy.
URSULA K. LE GUIN, in "The New Atlantis" (1975)

Lying is the misuse of language. We know that.
We need to remember that it works the other way round too.
Even with the best intentions, language misused,
language used stupidly, carelessly, brutally,
language used wrongly, breeds lies, half-truths, confusion.
URSULA LE GUIN, in *Steering the Craft* (1998)

A few years later, Le Guin expanded on this thought in an acceptance speech for the Maxine Cushing Gray Award (Oct. 18, 2006): "Evil government relies on deliberate misuse of language. Because literary skill is the rigorous use of language in the pursuit of truth, the habit of literature, of serious reading, is the best defense against believing the half-truths of ideologues and the lies of demagogues."

That's the way things come clear. All of a sudden.
And then you realize how obvious they've been all along.
MADELEINE L'ENGLE, in *The Arm of the Starfish* (1965)

We tend to think things are new
because we've just discovered them.
MADELEINE L'ENGLE, in *A Wind in the Door* (1973)

It's one thing to *think* things are new because you've only recently learned them, but Trump tends to think they're new to everyone else as well, as we see with his many "Most people don't know" or "People don't realize" utterances. For more on this strange personality quirk, see the Jean de La Bruyère entry above.

Truth is too weak to combat prejudice.
CHARLOTTE LENNOX, in *Henrietta* (1758)

We must rid ourselves of the view
that only logical ideas can be political weapons.
Ideas in politics are much like poetry;
they need no inner logical structure to be effective.
MAX LERNER, in Introduction to 1991 edition of
Ideas Are Weapons (1939)

What's terrible is to pretend
that the second-rate is first-rate.

DORIS LESSING, in *The Golden Notebook* (1962)

The words come from protagonist Anna Wulf, who is describing one of the great themes in her life as a writer and a woman. Later in the novel, she returns to the same topic, reflecting: "There's only one real sin, and that is to persuade oneself that the second-best is anything but the second-best."

Capable people do not understand incapacity;
clever people do not understand stupidity.

DORIS LESSING, in *Under My Skin* (1994)

We judge nothing so hastily as character,
and yet there is nothing over which
we should be more cautious.

G. C. LICHTENBERG, in *The Reflections of Lichtenberg* (1908)

Stand with anybody that stands *right*.
Stand with him while he is right,
and *part* with him when he goes wrong.

ABRAHAM LINCOLN, in speech in Peoria, IL (Oct. 16, 1854)

If a man says he *knows* a thing,
then he must show *how* he knows it.

ABRAHAM LINCOLN, in Lincoln-Douglas
Debate, Ottawa, IL (Aug. 21, 1858)

No party can command respect
which sustains this year what it opposed last.

ABRAHAM LINCOLN, in letter to Samuel Galloway (July 28, 1859)

He can compress the most words
into the smallest ideas
better than any man I ever met.
ABRAHAM LINCOLN, on a contemporary, quoted in
Frederick Trevor Hill, *Lincoln the Lawyer* (1906)

Like the famous quotation about fooling people some of the time and all of the time (which I discussed in the Franklin P. Adams entry earlier), this is yet another Lincoln quotation of questionable validity. I include it because it does seem relevant to Trump's frequent tendency to talk on and on without saying much of substance.

When one is a stranger to oneself
then one is estranged from others too.
If one is out of touch with oneself,
then one cannot touch others.
ANNE MORROW LINDBERGH, in *Gift from the Sea* (1955)

It isn't for the moment you are struck
that you need courage but for the long uphill climb
back to sanity and faith and security.
ANNE MORROW LINDBERGH, in *Hour of Gold, Hour of Lead* (1973)

Men who have lost their grip upon the
relevant facts of their environment are the
inevitable victims of agitation and propaganda.
The quack, the charlatan, the jingo, and the terrorist,
can flourish only where the audience
is deprived of independent access to information.
WALTER LIPPMANN, "What Modern Liberty
Means," in *Liberty and the News* (1920)

Lippmann seemed to be talking about our own time when he added: "But where all news comes at second-hand, where all the testimony is uncertain, men cease to respond to truth, and respond simply to opinions. The environment in which they act is not the realities themselves, but the pseudo-environment of reports, rumors, and guesses. The whole reference of thought comes to be what somebody asserts, not what actually is."

It is one thing to show a man that he is in error,
and another to put him in possession of the truth.
JOHN LOCKE, in *An Essay Concerning Human Understanding* (1690)

Crooked things may be as stiff and
unflexible [sic] as straight;
and men may be as positive in error as in truth.
JOHN LOCKE, in *An Essay Concerning Human Understanding* (1690)

All men are liable to error;
and most men are, in many points,
by passion or interest, under temptation to it.
JOHN LOCKE, in *An Essay Concerning Human Understanding* (1690)

There cannot be a greater rudeness than to
interrupt another in the current of his discourse.
JOHN LOCKE, in *Some Thoughts Concerning Education* (1693)

If you look at almost every Trump interview or press conference, you will notice that he rarely allows a journalist or interviewer to fully pose an extended question or make a comprehensive statement. From Locke's standpoint—and the position of most etiquette experts—interrupting someone in mid-sentence is an illustration of great rudeness. In the view of many observers, though, Trump interrupts not because he's rude, but because he wants to control the conversation. By dictating the terms of every interaction, he ensures that the dialogue is conducted on his terms and not the other person's. Later on, in the Thomas Sowell entry, you will also see how Trump's penchant for interrupting reflects an almost feral genius at manipulating face-to-face interactions to his advantage.

It is never right to compromise with dishonesty.
HENRY CABOT LODGE, Jr., quoted in R. N. Smith,
Thomas E. Dewey and His Times (1982)

Once to every man and nation comes
The moment to decide,
In the strife of Truth with Falsehood,
For the good or evil side.
JAMES RUSSELL LOWELL, in "The Present Crisis" (1844)

What generally passes for "thought" among
the majority of mankind is the time one takes
out to rearrange one's prejudices.
CLARE BOOTHE LUCE, quoted in *Today's Woman* (Apr. 1946)

In his classic *The American Treasury, 1455–1955* (1955), Clifton Fadiman made a rare mistake by quoting William James as saying: "A great many people think they are thinking when they are merely rearranging their prejudices." Fadiman didn't provide a source for the quotation, of course, because James never wrote or said anything like it. Luce is the original author of the sentiment.

There are no hopeless situations; there are only
people who have grown hopeless about them
CLARE BOOTH LUCE, in *Europe in the Spring* (1940)

A man should
be **upright,**
not be
kept **upright.**
Marcus Aurelius

**The doctrine which...has been held by all bigots
of all sects, when condensed into a few words
and stripped of rhetorical disguise, is simply this:
I am in the right, and you are in the wrong.**
THOMAS BABINGTON MACAULAY, in *Edinburgh Review* (July, 1835)

According to Macaulay, the bigot's doctrine continued this way:

"When you are the stronger, you ought to tolerate me, for
it is your duty to tolerate truth; but when I am the stronger,
I shall persecute you, for it is my duty to persecute error."

**In every age the vilest specimens of human nature
are to be found among demagogues.**
THOMAS BABINGTON MACAULAY, in *History of England* (1849)

**A prince who is not wise himself
will never take good advice.**
NICCOLÒ MACHIAVELLI, in *The Prince* (1532)

In a *Washington Post* article ("Donald Trump is the American
Machiavelli") written a week after the 2016 election, David Ignatius
wrote: "It's common to describe ruthless or devious politicians as
'Machiavellian.' But rarely in the United States have we seen an embod-
iment of the traits Machiavelli admired quite like Donald Trump, the
president-elect." It was quite a charge, and sent many to their favorite
reference sources to learn more about a man whose advice to leaders
included such pronouncements as, "It is much safer to be feared than
to be loved."

If Trump is, in fact, Machiavellian—and most agree he has those ten-
dencies—he's not a particularly good Machiavellian, for he ignores
much of the good advice that the author of *The Prince* did offer, including the admonition above about taking good advice.

The first method for estimating the intelligence of a ruler
is to look at the men he has around him.

NICCOLÒ MACHIAVELLI, in *The Prince* (1532)

While "Machiavellian" has become a synonym for devious and manipulative leaders, the eponym is now regarded as a bit of an oversimplifi-
cation, for *The Prince* also provided much sound advice, including this
observation about judging leaders on the basis of their aides, advisers,
and appointments. Trump's tendency to prefer hacks, loyalists, and
sycophants over competent professionals—along with his unwillingness to take advice, discussed above—must also be considered distinctly un-Machiavellian.

The entry above is a modern translation of Machiavelli's words, and
the one found in most current quotation anthologies. A century ago,
however, readers were more likely to see this fuller and more eloquently phrased version of the thought:

> "The first opinion which one forms of a prince, and of his
> understanding, is by observing the men he has around him;
> and when they are capable and faithful he may always be
> considered wise, because he has known how to recognize
> the capable and to keep them faithful. But when they are
> otherwise one cannot form a good opinion of him, for the
> prime error which he made was in choosing them."

The deceiver will never lack dupes.

NICCOLÒ MACHIAVELLI, in *The Prince* (1532)

The prince must be a lion,
But he must also know how to play the fox.

NICCOLÒ MACHIAVELLI, in *The Prince* (1532)

Those princes who have done great things
have held good faith of little account,
and have known how to circumvent
the intellect of men by craft,
and in the end have overcome those
who have relied on their word.

NICCOLÒ MACHIAVELLI, in *The Prince* (1532)

He who has known best how to employ
the [cunning of the] fox has succeeded best.
But it is necessary to know well how
to disguise this characteristic and
to be a great pretender and dissembler.

NICCOLÒ MACHIAVELLI, in *The Prince* (1532)

The several passages above reflect the kind of advice we most often associate with Machiavelli. In this last observation, he continued: "And men are so simple, and so subject to present necessities, that he who seeks to deceive will always find someone who will allow himself to be deceived."

The same fidelity to the public interest
which obliges those who are its appointed guardians,
to pursue with every vigor
a perfidious or dishonest servant of the public
requires them to confront the imputations
of malice against the good and faithful one.

JAMES MADISON, in letter to Edmund Randolph (June 4, 1782)

This may not be the most clearly phrased observation, but Madison's message is straightforward—public officials who behave badly must be vigorously confronted and the falsehoods they peddle about good officials must be staunchly opposed.

A bad cause seldom fails to betray itself.
JAMES MADISON, in *The Federalist Papers, No. 41* (Jan. 19, 1788)

Ambition is so vigilant, and...is so prompt in
seizing its advantages, that it cannot be
too closely watched or too vigorously checked.
JAMES MADISON, in letter to Thomas Jefferson (Dec. 25, 1797)

The essence of government is power, and power,
lodged as it must be in human hands,
will ever be liable to abuse.
JAMES MADISON, in speech at the Virginia Convention (Dec. 2, 1829)

After mentioning the abuses of power that have occurred in monarchies and aristocracies, Madison went on to write: "In Republics, the great danger is that the majority may not sufficiently respect the rights of the minority."

Every ignoramus imagines that all that exists,
exists with a view to his individual sake;
it is as if there were nothing that exists except him.
And if something happens to him that
is contrary to what he wishes,
he makes the trenchant judgment
that all that exists is an evil.
MAIMONIDES (Moses ben Maimon), in *The Guide for the Perplexed* (c. 1190)

This has long been my favorite description of the vast numbers of egocentric people in the world—Trump included—who believe the world revolves around them. In ancient Latin, *ignoramus* literally means "we do not know; we are ignorant of." When the word made its first appearance in English in a George Ruggle 1615 farce by that title, the meaning was extended to refer to an especially ignorant person. The term has been occasionally used to describe past US presidents, but the floodgates opened after the 2016 election, when it began to be routinely applied to Trump.

An early example occurred in 2012, a full three years before Trump launched his presidential campaign, when conservative columnist George F. Will grew concerned over the idea of GOP presidential candidate Mitt Romney appearing with Donald Trump at a Republican fundraiser. Questioning the wisdom of an establishment Republican sharing the stage with the most vocal proponent of the "birther" movement, Will said on an ABC-TV *This Week* broadcast: "The cost of appearing with this bloviating ignoramus is obvious, it seems to me. Donald Trump is redundant evidence that if your net worth is high enough, your IQ can be very low and you can still intrude into American politics."

The second, from firebrand conservative Ann Coulter, was a bit more surprising. Coulter was an early and avid Trump supporter, even writing a 2016 campaign book titled *In Trump We Trust*. As his presidency unfolded, though, Coulter became less and less enamored, even confessing in a March 2018 forum at Columbia University, "I knew he was a shallow, lazy ignoramus, and I didn't care."

The biggest liar in the world is They Say.
DOUGLAS MALLOCH, "The Truth About Truth," *Judge* (Dec. 21, 1978)

**An individualism which has got
beyond the stage of hedonism
tends to yield to the lure of the grandiose.**
ANDRÉ MALRAUX, in *The Voices of Silence* (1951)

If someone is able to show me
that what I think or do is not right,
I will happily change, for I seek the truth,
by which no one ever was truly harmed.
Harmed is the person who continues
in his self-deception and ignorance.

MARCUS AURELIUS, in *Meditations* (2nd c. AD)

This was an entry in the diary of the most philosophically inclined of all Roman emperors, a ruler who considered himself a follower of the Stoic philosopher Epictetus. The personal journal of Marcus Aurelius was discovered after his death at age fifty-eight in AD 180, and eventually published under the title *Meditations*. It went on to become one of history's most influential books and—with the possible exception of Donald Trump—every major leader in world history has had at least a passing acquaintance with it. The book contains many timeless and Trump-relevant passages:

Our life is what our thoughts make it.

The soul is dyed by the color of its thoughts.

If it is not right, don't do it; if it is not true, don't say it.

That which is not good for the hive is not good for the bee.

It is man's peculiar duty to love even those who wrong him.

Waste no more time arguing what
a good man should be. Be one.

If a man is mistaken, instruct him
kindly and show him his error.

Be not careless in deeds, nor confused
in words, nor rambling in thought.

Blot out vain pomp; check impulse; quench
appetite; keep reason under its own control.

> Soon you will have forgotten the world,
> and soon the world will have forgotten you.

Never esteem anything as of advantage to you that will
make you break your word or lose your self-respect.

> Remember this—that there is a proper
> dignity and proportion to be observed
> in the performance of every act of life.

A man should *be* upright,
not be *kept* upright.

This final Marcus Aurelius quotation about a person in need of being *kept upright* is at the heart of one of the most intriguing metaphors of the Trump presidency—the importance of having "adults in the room" to prevent a US president from acting on his worst impulses. The metaphor (often phrased as *grownups in the room*) was especially interesting when it was employed by Trump supporters, for it represented a tacit admission that they agreed with the underlying notion that safeguards needed to be put in place to protect American citizens from decisions by someone who couldn't be trusted to act in the best interests of the nation.

> **It is far more impressive when others
> discover your good qualities without your help.**
> JUDITH MARTIN ("Miss Manners"), in 1991 issue of *Cosmopolitan*

The whole country wants civility.
Why don't we have it? It doesn't cost anything.
No federal funding, no legislation is involved.
One answer is the unwillingness to restrain oneself.
Everybody wants other people to be polite to them,
but they want the freedom
of not having to be polite to others.

JUDITH MARTIN ("Miss Manners"),
in *Psychology Today* (Mar. 1, 1998)

You can't have one kind of man and
another kind of President.

LYNN MORLEY MARTIN, in speech at Republican
National Convention (Aug. 18, 1992)

It is cruel to discover one's mediocrity
only when it is too late.

W. SOMERSET MAUGHAM, in *Of Human Bondage* (1915)

Like all weak men he laid an exaggerated stress
on not changing one's mind.

W. SOMERSET MAUGHAM, in *Of Human Bondage* (1915)

To acquire the habit of reading is to construct for yourself
a refuge from almost all the miseries of life.

W. SOMERSET MAUGHAM, in *Books and You* (1940)

To reason with poorly chosen words
is like using a pair of scales with inaccurate weights.

ANDRÉ MAUROIS, in *The Art of Living* (1939)

We may be accessory to another's sin
by counsel, by command, by consent,
by concealment, by provoking, by praise,
by partaking, by silence, by defense.

JOHN MCCAFFREY, in *A Catechism of Christian Doctrine* (1866)

The know-nothings are, unfortunately,
seldom the do-nothings.

MIGNON MCLAUGHLIN, in *The Neurotic's Notebook* (1963)

Incompetents invariably make trouble
for people other than themselves.

LARRY MCMURTRY, in *Lonesome Dove* (1985)

As democracy is perfected, the office [of US president]
represents more and more closely,
the inner soul of the people.
On some great and glorious day, the plain folks
of the land will reach their heart's desire at last, and
the White House will be adorned by a downright moron.

H. L. MENCKEN, "Bayard v. Lionheart," in
The Baltimore Evening Sun (July 26, 1920)

This quotation—or more precisely, an inaccurately phrased version of this quotation—was circulating all over the internet just after Trump's surprising victory in the 2016 election. As I discussed in the Introduction, it was one of the early quotations I included in a computer file I'd recently created for new Trump-related quotations.

Man is the yokel *par excellence,*
the booby unmatchable, the king dupe of the cosmos.
He is chronically and unescapably deceived, not only by
the other animals and by the delusive face of nature herself,
but also and more particularly by himself—
by his incomparable talent for searching out
and embracing what is false,
and for overlooking and denying what is true.

H. L. MENCKEN, in *Prejudices: Third Series* (1922)

The whole aim of practical politics is
to keep the populace alarmed
(and hence clamorous to be led to safety)
by menacing it with an endless series of
hobgoblins, all of them imaginary.

H. L. MENCKEN, in *In Defense of Women* (1923)

A selfish love of ourselves makes us
incapable of loving others.

THOMAS MERTON, in *No Man is an Island* (1955)

We stumble and fall constantly
even when we are most enlightened.
But when we are in true spiritual darkness,
we do not even know that we have fallen.

THOMAS MERTON, in *Thoughts in Solitude* (1956)

M. Scott Peck was almost certainly influenced by this famous Merton observation when he wrote in *The Road Less Traveled* (1978): "We are most often in the dark when we are the most certain, and the most enlightened when we are the most confused."

We are not very good at recognizing illusions,
least of all the ones we cherish about ourselves.

THOMAS MERTON, in *New Seeds of Contemplation* (1962)

How easy it is, how dangerously easy it is
to hate a man for one's own inadequacies.

GRACE METALIOUS, in *Peyton Place* (1956)

Religion is like music,
one must have an ear for it.
Some people have none at all.

CHARLOTTE MEW, in P. Fitzgerald, *Charlotte
Mew and Her Friends* (1984)

It is not because men's desires are strong that they act ill;
it is because their consciences are weak.

JOHN STUART MILL, in *On Liberty* (1859)

A person may cause evil to others
not only by his actions but by his inaction,
and in either case he is justly accountable
to them for the injury.

JOHN STUART MILL, in *On Liberty* (1859)

Bad men need nothing more to compass their ends
than that good men should look on and do nothing.

JOHN STUART MILL, in "On Education," his inaugural
address as rector of St. Andrews (Feb. 1, 1867)

This observation is the likely inspiration for one of history's most
famous apocryphal quotations, almost always attributed to Edmund

Burke, but never found in his writings: "The only thing necessary for the triumph of evil is that good men do nothing."

It's likely that William Sloane Coffin was inspired by one or both of these quotations when he wrote in *Once to Every Man: A Memoir* (1977): "In our time all it takes for evil to flourish is for a few good men to be a little wrong and have a great deal of power, and for the vast majority of their fellow citizens to remain indifferent."

<blockquote>
A stupid person's notions and feelings
may confidently be inferred
from those which prevail in the circle
by which the person is surrounded.

JOHN STUART MILL, in *The Subjection of Women* (1869)
</blockquote>

<blockquote>
No great improvements in the lot of mankind
are possible until a great change takes place
in the fundamental constitution
of their modes of thought.

JOHN STUART MILL, in *Autobiography* (1873)
</blockquote>

<blockquote>
The grandiose person is never really free...
because he is excessively dependent
on admiration from others.

ALICE MILLER, in *The Drama of the Gifted Child* (1997)
</blockquote>

<blockquote>
Lord, there's danger in this land
You get witch-hunts and wars
When church and state hold hands.

JONI MITCHELL, in *Both Sides Now* (a 1992 illustrated book)
</blockquote>

It had been her experience that
the liar was the hottest to defend his veracity,
the coward his courage,
the ill-bred his gentlemanliness,
and the cad his honor.

MARGARET MITCHELL, describing the experience of
Scarlett O'Hara, in *Gone with the Wind* (1936)

Those who have greatest cause for guilt and shame
Are quickest to besmirch a neighbor's name.
When there's a chance for libel, they never miss it;
When something can be made to seem illicit
They're off at once to spread the joyous news,
Adding to fact what fantasies they choose.
By talking up their neighbor's indiscretions
They seek to camouflage their own transgressions,
Hoping that others' innocent affairs
Will lend a hue of innocence to theirs,
Or that their own black guilt will come to seem
Part of a general shady color-scheme.

MOLIÈRE (Jean-Baptiste Poquelin), in *Tartuffe* (1664)

The words come from the character Dorine, who is speaking about the slanderous tongue of her rival, Daphne. It was the discovery of this literary treasure in the summer of 2015 that set in motion a chain of events that eventually resulted in this book. For more, see my discussion of the passage in the Introduction.

People can be induced to swallow anything,
provided it is sufficiently seasoned with praise.

MOLIÈRE (Jean-Baptiste Poquelin), in *The Miser* (1668)

This is a modern translation, slightly different from traditional translations, which presented the passage this way: "However gross the

flattery, the most cunning are easily duped; there is nothing so imper-
tinent or ridiculous which they will not believe, provided it be seasoned with praise."

**Attacks on me will do no harm,
and silent contempt is the best answer to them.**

JAMES MONROE, in letter to George Hay (Apr. 29, 1808)

**A little flattery will support
a man through great fatigue.**

JAMES MONROE, in letter to F. A. Van Der Kemp (Jan. 24, 1818)

**We are all liable to error, and those who
are engaged in the management of public affairs
are more subject to excitement and to be led astray
by their particular interests and passions
than the great body of our constituents.**

JAMES MONROE, in seventh annual message
to Congress (Dec. 2, 1823)

**People are never so near playing the fool
as when they think themselves wise.**

LADY MARY WORTLEY MONTAGU, in letter
to her daughter (Mar. 1, 1755)

**A man's accusations of himself
are always believed; his praises never.**

MICHEL DE MONTAIGNE, "Of the Art of
Conference," in Essays (1580–1588)

Since we cannot attain to greatness,
let us revenge ourselves by railing at it.

MICHEL DE MONTAIGNE, "Of the Inconvenience
of Greatness," in Essays (1580–1588)

It's possible that Edgar Allen Poe was influenced by this popular Montaigne observation when he wrote in *Marginalia* (1844): "To vilify a great man is the readiest way in which a little man can himself attain greatness."

It is not only crimes that destroy virtue, but also negligence,
mistakes, certain slackness in the love of the homeland,
dangerous examples, the seeds of corruption,
that which does not run counter to the laws but eludes them,
that which does not destroy them but weakens them.

CHARLES DE MONTESQUIEU, in The Spirit of the Laws (1748)

Study has been my sovereign remedy
against the worries of life.
I have never had a care that an hour's
reading could not dispel.

CHARLES DE MONTESQUIEU, in My Thoughts, 1720-55

Who flatters is of all mankind the lowest,
Save he who courts flattery.

HANNAH MORE, in Sacred Dramas (1782)

There are certain faults which press
too near our self-love to be even perceptible to us.

HANNAH MORE, in Thoughts on the Importance of the
Manners of the Great to General Society (1788)

The ingenuity of self-deception is inexhaustible.

HANNAH MORE, "Self-Love," in *Practical Piety* (1811)

There is scarcely any fault in another
which offends us more than vanity,
though perhaps there is none
that really injures us so little.

HANNAH MORE, "Self-Love," in *Practical Piety* (1811)

No man can climb out beyond
the limitations of his own character.

JOHN MORLEY, "Robespierre," in *Critical Miscellanies* (1886)

We must not confuse dissent with disloyalty.

EDWARD R. MURROW, "See It Now," CBS-TV Broadcast (Mar. 7, 1954)

This legendary television broadcast, formally titled "Report on Sen. Joseph R. McCarthy," was the first major domino to fall in the eventual toppling of the right-wing demagogue from Wisconsin. In *The Oxford Dictionary of American Quotations* (2006), Hugh Rawson and Margaret Miner wrote: "This was the first major assault on McCarthyism. Even the popular and influential Murrow felt that he had to bide his time until McCarthy's excesses began to worry the American public."

To be fair, other prominent figures had previously denounced McCarthy (President Truman called him "a pathological character assassin" in 1952), but it was Murrow's broadcast that seemed to embolden other Americans. Three months later, in the televised "Army-McCarthy" hearings, attorney Joseph Welch famously said to the Wisconsin senator: "Have you no sense of decency, sir, at long last? Have you no sense of decency?"

No one can terrorize a whole nation,
unless we are all his accomplices.

EDWARD R. MURROW, on Sen. Joseph McCarthy, "See
It Now" CBS-TV broadcast (Mar. 7, 1954)

In the broadcast, Murrow added a comment about McCarthy that seems equally true about Donald Trump: "He didn't create this situation of fear. He merely exploited it, and rather successfully."

Resentment isn't
a magnetic
personal style.

Peggy Noonan

**There is only one step
from the sublime to the ridiculous.**
NAPOLEON I, an 1812 remark after his retreat from Russia

**When small men attempt great enterprises,
they always end by
reducing them to the level of their mediocrity.**
NAPOLEON I, in J. Bertaut, *Napoleon in His Own Words* (1916)

A leader is a dealer in hope.
NAPOLEON I, in J. Bertaut, *Napoleon in His Own Words* (1916)

The notion that a leader is *a dealer in hope* has been around for many years, but it skyrocketed in popularity after Barack Obama made *the audacity of hope* the centerpiece of his 2008 presidential campaign. Obama introduced the phrase four years earlier in his keynote address at the Democratic National Convention, and he used it to title a 2006 book that signaled his intention to run for president.

While liberals are reluctant to describe Donald Trump as a dealer in hope, he has clearly played that role with his core constituencies, including disenfranchised white males without college degrees, evangelical Christians and others in the religious right, members of what has become known as the alt-right, and, finally, white nationalists like David Duke, who said during the 2016 campaign: "Voting against Donald Trump at this point is really treason to your heritage."

**I cannot help mentioning that
the door of a bigoted mind opens outwards
so that the only result of the pressure of facts
upon it is to close it more snugly.**
OGDEN NASH, in *Good Intentions* (1942)

Bad officials are elected by good citizens who do not vote.

GEORGE JEAN NATHAN, quoted in Clifton Fadiman,
The American Treasury (1955)

True strength is delicate.

LOUISE NEVELSON, in A. Glimcher, *Louise Nevelson* (1972)

A valuable qualification of a modern politician
seems to be a capacity for
concealing or explaining away the truth.

DOROTHY NEVILL, in *My Own Times* (1912)

We can believe what we choose.
We are answerable for what we choose to believe.

JOHN HENRY NEWMAN, in letter to Mrs.
William Froude (June 27, 1848)

Moreover, there is this harm too, and one of vast extent...
that by insincerity and lying, faith and truth are lost,
which are the firmest bonds of human society,
and, when they are lost, supreme confusion follows in life,
so that men seem in nothing to differ from devils.

JOHN HENRY NEWMAN, in *Apologia Pro Vita Sua* (1864)

It is almost a definition of a gentleman
to say that he is one who never inflicts pain.

JOHN HENRY NEWMAN, in *The Idea of a University* (1873)

If you equate God's judgment with your judgment,
you have a wrong religion.

REINHOLD NIEBUHR, in ABC-TV interview (Apr. 27, 1958)

The whole art of politics consists in
directing rationally the irrationalities of man.

REINHOLD NIEBUHR, quoted in *New York*
Times obituary (June 2, 1971)

Convictions are more dangerous enemies of truth than lies.

FRIEDRICH NIETZSCHE, in *Human, All Too Human* (1878)

One will rarely err if extreme actions be ascribed to vanity,
ordinary actions to habit, and mean actions to fear.

FRIEDRICH NIETZSCHE, in *Human, All Too Human* (1878)

An excellent quotation can annihilate entire pages,
indeed an entire book, in that it warns the reader
and seems to cry out to him: "Beware, I am the jewel..."

FRIEDRICH NIETZSCHE, in *Human, All Too Human* (1878)

Distrust all in whom the impulse to punish is powerful.

FRIEDRICH NIETZSCHE, in *Thus Spake Zarathustra* (1883)

The most common sort of lie is the one uttered to one's self.

FRIEDRICH NIETZSCHE, in *The Antichrist* (1888)

No one is such a liar as the indignant man.

FRIEDRICH NIETZSCHE, in *Beyond Good and Evil* (1886)

Whoever fights monsters should see to it that
in the process he does not become a monster.

FRIEDRICH NIETZSCHE, in *Beyond Good and Evil* (1886)

This is one of Nietzsche's most celebrated observations. He concluded by writing: "And when you look long into an abyss, the abyss also
looks into you."

Willingness to explore everything
is a sign of strength.
The weak ones have prejudices.
Prejudices are a protection.

ANAÏS NIN, a 1933 diary entry

The press is the enemy.

RICHARD M. NIXON, quoted by William
Safire, in *Before the Fall* (1975)

I played by the rules of politics as I found them.
Not taking a higher road than my predecessors
and my adversaries was my central mistake.

RICHARD M. NIXON, in *In the Arena* (1990)

True religion is the life we lead,
not the creed we profess.

LOUIS NIZER, in *Reflections Without Mirrors* (1978)

A graceful taunt is worth a thousand insults.

LOUIS NIZER, quoted by the Associated Press in 1973

I've been surprised that the targets of Trump's insults over the years
have been so ineffective in their replies. The key to responding effec-
tively is not to "fight fire with fire," but to reply with wit and clever-
ness—in essence, to let the *bigness* of the reply reveal the *littleness* of
Trump. One of my objectives in publishing this anthology is to provide raw material for speechwriters and campaign advisers whose job

it is to supply their candidates with *graceful taunts.* Let me offer just one example.

Imagine you're the next Democratic nominee for president, and Trump has just tweeted some lie about you. When a journalist asks for your reaction, how do you respond? Do you say it's just another Trump lie, one of the thousands he's tweeted? Do you say that Trump is a pathological liar, as Bernie Sanders has said on so many occasions? Or do you look the interviewer in the eye and calmly reply, "Your question brings to mind a Virginia Woolf quotation: "If you do not tell the truth about yourself, you cannot tell it about other people." Since Mr. Trump has gone to all the best schools, I'm sure he's familiar with Virginia Woolf, so ask him about it sometime."

Resentment isn't a magnetic personal style.

PEGGY NOONAN, in *What I Saw at the Revolution* (1990)

Beware the politically obsessed.
They are often bright and interesting,
but they have something missing
in their natures; there is a hole, an empty place,
and they use politics to fill it up.
It leaves them somehow misshapen.

PEGGY NOONAN, in *What I Saw at the Revolution* (1990)

If we do not always see our own mistakes and omissions
we can always see those of our neighbors.

KATHLEEN THOMPSON NORRIS, in *Hands Full of Living* (1931)

[He] was his own world,
and nothing that concerned anyone
else was important to him...
and nothing that touched him unimportant.

KATHLEEN THOMPSON NORRIS, in *Walls of Gold* (1933)

This description of a character in Norris's novel perfectly lays out the *modus operandi* of the narcissist: "If it's not about me, it's not important; if it is, it is."

The lover of books is a miner,
searching for gold all his life long.
He finds his nuggets, his heart leaps in his breast;
he cannot believe in his good fortune.
Traversing a slow page, to come upon
a lode of the pure shining metal
is to exult inwardly for greedy hours.

KATHLEEN THOMPSON NORRIS, in *These I Like Best* (1941)

If you asked me to describe what it was like to search for—and find—the quotations that make up this anthology, I couldn't find words any better than those Norris uses here.

The voice of protest, of warning, of appeal is never
more needed than when the clamor of fife and drum,
echoed by the press and too often by the pulpit
is bidding all men to fall in and keep step and
obey in silence the tyrannous word of command.
Then, more than ever,
it is the duty of the good citizen not to be silent.

CHARLES ELIOT NORTON, in *True Patriotism* (1898)

**The truth
does not change
according to
our ability to
stomach it emotionally.**

Flannery O'Connor

Perhaps evil isn't a cosmological riddle,
only just selfish human behavior,
and this behavior the result of
conscious, accountable choice.

JOYCE CAROL OATES, "Crime and Punishment," in
The New York Times (Sep. 19, 1999)

Those whom the gods wish to destroy,
they first make famous.

JOYCE CAROL OATES, "Down the Road," in
The New Yorker (Mar. 27, 1985)

The blow you can't see coming is the blow
that knocks you out—the blow out of nowhere.

JOYCE CAROL OATES, "Golden Gloves," in *Raven's Wing* (1985)

The truth does not change according to
our ability to stomach it emotionally.

FLANNERY O'CONNOR, in a 1955 letter

Those who would renegotiate the boundaries
between church and state must therefore
answer a difficult question:
Why would we trade a system that has served us so well
for one that has served others so poorly?

SANDRA DAY O'CONNOR, in *McCreary County
v. A.C.L.U. of Kentucky* (2005)

Hot lead can be almost as effective
coming from a linotype as from a firearm

JOHN O'HARA, in Introduction to *The Portable
F. Scott Fitzgerald* (1945)

Newspapers no longer use linotype, but O'Hara's observation remains as true today as when it was first written.

A man morally small resembles a statue in this respect: the higher he is elevated, the more he dwindles.
AUSTIN O'MALLEY, in *Keystones of Thought* (1914)

O'Malley is not well remembered today, but he was something of a Renaissance Man in his lifetime. A child prodigy, he was fourteen when he entered Fordham University and ultimately graduated at the head of his class. He went on to combine a medical/scientific career with his interest in literature, even serving for a number of years as an English professor at Notre Dame University. In addition to his medical and scientific contributions, which were substantial, he became popular for books like *Thoughts of a Recluse* (1898) and *Keystones of Thought* (1914), a book of his aphorisms. Many thoughts from the *Keystones* book bear on our current subject, including the one above on morally small men, and the brief sampling that follow:

The ass that brays is not working.

He that is always right is always wrong.

A cocksure man is either a lunatic or a fool.

A poor surgeon never can get a good scalpel.

When you throw mud, you befoul your own hand.

It is twice as hard to crush a half-truth as a whole lie.

If you handle truth carelessly, it will cut your fingers.

Those that admire strength in a rascal do not live in his town.

In dealing with a foolish or stubborn adversary remember your own mood constitutes half the force opposing you.

The President might be a real tightwad
when it comes to programs that help working families,
but when it comes to giving tax breaks
to the wealthy of this country,
the President has a heart of gold

THOMAS P. ("TIP") O'NEILL, on Ronald Reagan,
quoted in a 1981 issue of *Time*

Our own political life is predicated on openness.
We do not believe any group of men
adequate enough or wise enough
to operate without scrutiny or without criticism.

J. ROBERT OPPENHEIMER, "Encouragement of Science,"
address at Science Talent Institute (Mar. 6, 1950)

Oppenheimer added: "We know that the only way to avoid error is to detect it, that the only way to detect it is to be free to inquire. We know that the wages of secrecy are corruption. We know that in secrecy error, undetected, will flourish and subvert."

Humor gives presidents the chance
to be seen as warm, relaxed persons.
Humor reaches out and puts its arm
around the listener and says,
"I am one of you, I understand," and implicitly it promises,
"I will do something about your problems."

ROBERT ORBEN, in *The Toronto Star* (Sep. 21, 1986)

In 1968, Gerald Ford, a Republican congressman with a reputation for being dull, hired Orben, a popular joke writer, for an upcoming Gridiron Club dinner. At the event, Ford's humor-laced speech was the surprise highlight of the evening. Orben went on to become a Ford speechwriter, penning his famous "I'm a Ford, not a Lincoln" line.

Many observers have commented on Trump's lack of a sense of humor, with some even suggesting he's *devoid of humor* or *unfunny*. In a *New York Times* column titled "A Presidency Without Humor" (Dec. 7, 2018), columnist Bret Stephens took it a step further, describing Trump as "anti-funny." Stephens wrote: "Humor humanizes. It uncorks, unstuffs, informalizes. Used well, it puts people at ease. Trump's method is the opposite: He wants people ill at ease. Doing so preserves his capacity to wound, his sense of superiority, his distance. Good jokes highlight the ridiculous. Trump's jokes merely ridicule."

> **Authority has always attracted**
> **the lowest elements in the human race.**
> P. J. O'ROURKE, in *Parliament of Whores* (1991)

O'Rourke continued: "All through history mankind has been bullied by scum. Those who lord it over their fellows and toss commands in every direction and would boss the grass in the meadow about which way to bend in the wind are the most depraved kind of prostitutes. They will submit to any indignity, perform any vile act, do anything to achieve power."

> **No drug, not even alcohol,**
> **causes the fundamental ills of society.**
> **If we're looking for the source of our troubles,**
> **we shouldn't test people for drugs, we should test them**
> **for stupidity, ignorance, greed, and love of power.**
> P. J. O'ROURKE, in *Give War a Chance* (1992)

When one watches some tired hack on the platform
mechanically repeating the familiar phrases...
one often has a curious feeling that one is not watching
a live human being but some kind of dummy....
A speaker...turning himself into a machine.

GEORGE ORWELL, "Politics and the English
Language" in *Horizon* (Apr. 1946)

It was in the same essay—the most celebrated of all Orwell's essays—
that he offered some of his most famous observations. They include:

The great enemy of clear language is insincerity.

If thought corrupts language,
language can also corrupt thought.

Orthodoxy, of whatever color, seems
to demand a lifeless, imitative style.

In our age there is no such thing
as "keeping out of politics."
All issues are political issues.

Political language...is designed to make
lies sound truthful and murder respectable,
and to give an appearance of solidity to pure wind.

The English language...becomes ugly and
inaccurate because our thoughts are foolish,
but the slovenliness of our language makes it
easier for us to have foolish thoughts.

By "patriotism" I mean devotion to
a particular place and a particular way of life,
which one believes to be the best in the world
but has no wish to force on other people.

GEORGE ORWELL, "Notes on Nationalism," in *Polemic* (Oct. 1945)

Orwell's essay was written just as World War II was coming to an end, but his observations seem as relevant today as when they were originally written.

In stark contrast to patriotism, Orwell believed that nationalism was "inseparable from the desire for power." He went on to add: "The abiding purpose of every nationalist is to secure more power and more prestige, not for himself but for the nation...in which he has chosen to sink his own individuality." Here are some other quotations from the essay:

Nationalism is power hunger tempered by self-deception.

If one harbors anywhere in one's mind a
nationalistic loyalty or hatred, certain facts
although...known to be true, are inadmissible.

The nationalist not only does not disapprove
of atrocities committed by his own side,
but he has a remarkable capacity
for not even hearing about them.

By "nationalism" I mean...the habit of
identifying oneself with a single nation...
placing it beyond good and evil and recognizing
no other duty than that of advancing its interests.

Nationalism is not to be confused with patriotism.
Both words are normally used in so vague a way
that...one must draw a distinction between them,
since two different and opposing ideas are involved.

Intensely selfish people are always
very decided as to what they wish.
That is in itself a great force:
they do not waste their energies in
considering the good of others.

OUIDA, in *Wanda, Countess von Szalras* (1883)

There is nothing that you may
not get people to believe in
if you will only tell it them
loud enough and often enough.

OUIDA, in *Wisdom, Wit, and Pathos* (1884)

**There is
no such thing
as a minor
lapse of integrity.**

Tom Peters

These are the times that try men's souls
THOMAS PAINE, first line of "The American Crisis," in
The Pennsylvania Journal (Dec. 19, 1776)

These are the opening words of the first of sixteen pamphlets Paine published between 1776 and 1783. Paine was well known in colonial America for his writings in support of the Revolutionary cause, but he became enshrined in American history when, four days after these words first appeared in print, George Washington read the entire pamphlet to his battle-weary, half-frozen Continental Army troops on December 23, 1776.

General Washington's purpose was to raise the morale of his troops, and it worked. Three days later, they crossed the Delaware River and emerged victorious in the Battle of Trenton. Paine's legendary words have been recalled many times in American history—and they began to enjoy a renewed popularity after Trump's 2016 electoral victory.

A bad cause will ever be supported
by bad means and bad men.
THOMAS PAINE, in "The American Crisis, No. 2" (Jan. 13, 1777)

In 1774, Paine emigrated to America with the assistance of Benjamin Franklin, who he had met a few years earlier in London, and it wasn't long before he got caught up in the revolutionary fervor. In January of 1776, he published "Common Sense," a pamphlet advocating independence from Great Britain. With royalties going to George Washington's Continental Army, the pamphlet provided valuable financial assistance, but there is no evidence to support the popular claim that it sold a half-million copies.

Paine is often omitted from lists of America's Founding Fathers, but there are many who believe the country would not have come into being without his assistance. In an 1819 letter to Thomas Jefferson,

John Adams wrote, "History is to ascribe the American Revolution to Thomas Paine."

A narrow system of politics,
like a narrow system of religion,
is calculated only to sour the temper,
and live at variance with mankind.

THOMAS PAINE, in "The American Crisis, No. 3" (Apr. 19, 1777)

Silence becomes a kind of crime when it operates as
a cover or an encouragement to the guilty.

THOMAS PAINE, in *Pennsylvania Packet* (Jan. 23, 1779)

Character is much easier kept than recovered.

THOMAS PAINE, in "The American Crisis, No. 13" (Apr. 19, 1783)

There are two distinct species of popularity:
the one excited by merit, the other by resentment.

THOMAS PAINE, in *The Rights of Man* (1791)

When the tongue or the pen is let loose
in a frenzy of passion, it is the man,
and not the subject, that becomes exhausted.

THOMAS PAINE, in *The Rights of Man* (1791)

This observation helped me view Trump's Twitter habit in a new way—and it provided a wonderful phrase ("frenzy of passion") to describe his "tweet storms." In general, when people are in a frenzy of passion, the job of a leader is to dampen the flames so that cooler heads will prevail. When leaders are in a frenzy of passion, however, it is the people who become concerned.

After a particularly troubling flurry of tweets and re-tweets in March of 2019, George Conway, a conservative lawyer, frequent Trump critic, and husband of Kellyanne Conway, simply tweeted: "His condition is getting worse." Conway also re-tweeted Bill Kristol's analysis of the president's Twitter rampage:

> "To Republicans who've been inclined to acquiesce in a Trump re-nomination in 2020: Read his tweets this morning. Think seriously about his mental condition and psychological state. Then tell me you're fine with him as president of the United States for an additional four years."

Reason obeys itself;
and ignorance submits to whatever is dictated to it.

THOMAS PAINE, in *The Rights of Man* (1791)

Infidelity does not consist in believing or in disbelieving;
it consists in professing to believe what he does not believe.

THOMAS PAINE, in *The Age of Reason* (1794)

Errors, or caprices of the temper,
can be pardoned and forgotten,
but a cold, deliberate crime of the heart...
is not to be washed away.

THOMAS PAINE, in letter to George
Washington (Feb. 22, 1795)

When moral principles, rather than persons,
are candidates for power, to vote is to perform
a moral duty, and not to vote is to neglect a duty.

THOMAS PAINE, quoted in the Trenton
[New Jersey] *True-American* (Apr. 1803)

Where there is no danger, cowards are bold.
THOMAS PAINE, in an open letter to U.S. citizens (May 14, 1803)

In televised remarks from the White House on February 27, 2018, less than two weeks after the school shooting at Marjory Stoneman Douglas High School in Parkland, Florida, Trump said it was "a disgrace" and "frankly disgusting" that an armed school officer failed to rush toward the sound of a firing assault rifle during the attack. In his remarks, Trump also said: "You don't know until you're tested, but I think I—I really believe I'd run in there even if I didn't have a weapon."

From the moment we expect gratitude, we forfeit it.
IVAN PANIN, in *Thoughts* (1886)

If you want people to think well of you,
do not speak well of yourself
BLAISE PASCAL, in *Pensées* (1670)

A man never reveals his character more vividly
than when portraying the character of another.
JEAN PAUL (pen name of Johann Paul Richter), in *Titan* (1803)

Human beings are poor examiners,
subject to superstition, bias, prejudice, and a
profound tendency to see what they want to see
rather than what is really there.
M. SCOTT PECK, in *The Road Less Traveled* (1978)

Difficult though integrity may be to achieve,
the test for it is deceptively simple.
If you wish to discern either the
presence or absence of integrity,
you need to ask only one question.
What is missing? Has anything been left out?
M. SCOTT PECK, in *The Different Drum* (1987)

The major threats to our survival no longer
stem from nature without but from
our own human nature within.
It is our carelessness, our hostilities, our selfishness
and pride and willful ignorance that endanger the world.
M. SCOTT PECK, in *People of the Lie* (1983)

He who does not bellow the truth when he knows the truth
makes himself the accomplice of liars and forgers.
CHARLES PÉGUY, in "Lettre du Provincial" (Dec. 21, 1899)

To be a man's own fool is bad enough;
but the vain man is everybody's.
WILLIAM PENN, in *Some Fruits of Solitude* (1693)

In 1682, 38-year-old William Penn was better known as the son of a famous British admiral when he sailed to the American colonies in search of religious freedom (a convert to Quakerism, he had been expelled from Oxford for rejecting Anglicanism, and even imprisoned a number of times for his heresy). Upon his arrival, Penn took possession of a vast tract of land that King Charles II had granted to his father. Penn originally wanted to call the new province Sylvania (Latin for "forested land"), but King Charles formally changed it to Pennsylvania ("Penn's land") to further honor the memory of Penn's father (the decision was reluctantly accepted by the younger Penn, who feared people would think he named the new colony for himself).

As the province's first governor, Penn wrote a constitution that included many features that would later show up in the US Constitution: an amending clause (the first ever), a separation of powers clause, a right to trial by jury, and a degree of religious freedom that made the colony a refuge for Quakers, Jews, and other oppressed religious groups.

In his lifetime, Penn was a prolific writer, producing scores of books and pamphlets. His 1682 book *No Cross, No Crown*, originally written during his imprisonment in the Tower of London, is one of history's great examples of prison literature. *Some Fruits of Solitude*, a 1693 collection of philosophical reflections and moral observations greatly influenced the thinking of the Founding Fathers—and are as relevant today as when they were originally written. Here's a sampling with particular relevance to the Trump Era:

Inquiry is human, blind obedience, brutal.

We are too apt to love praise, but not to deserve it.

They have a right to censure, that have a heart to help.

Refuse not to be informed: for that shows pride or stupidity.

They must first judge themselves,
that presume to censure others.

Truth often suffers more by the heat of its
defenders than from the arguments of its opposers.

There is a troublesome humor some men have,
that if they may not lead, they will not follow.

In all debates let truth be thy aim;
not victory or an unjust interest; and endeavor
to gain rather than to expose thy antagonist.

Believe nothing against another, but upon good authority:
nor report what may hurt another,
unless it be a greater hurt to others to conceal it.

Everyone has his vanity, and each one's vanity
is his forgetting that there are others with an equal soul.
FERNANDO PESSOA, in *The Book of Disquiet* (1982)

In a hierarchy every employee
tends to rise to his level of incompetence.
LAURENCE J. PETER, in *The Peter Principle* (1969; with Raymond Hull)

There is no such thing as a minor lapse of integrity.
TOM PETERS, in *The Tom Peters Seminar* (1994)

In architecture and engineering, a structure is said to have "integrity" when it is designed and constructed in such a way that it will not fail under undue stress. A bridge with structural integrity, for example, will be able to tolerate heavy loads without crumbling. Conversely, a building lacking in structural integrity will suffer catastrophic consequences during, say, a hurricane or tornado.

The concept of structural integrity can be easily extended to individuals. A person with a good character structure is able to withstand temptation or tolerate the ethical stressors typically associated with fame, power, wealth, or celebrity. When candidate Trump formally bragged in the *Access Hollywood* tape about what his celebrity status allowed him to do with women, he wasn't simply describing a lapse in integrity, he was revealing a structural flaw.

> **Any effort that has self-glorification**
> **as its final endpoint is bound to end in disaster.**
>
> ROBERT M. PIRSIG, in *Zen and the Art of*
> *Motorcycle Maintenance* (1974)

Pirsig went on to add: "When you try to climb a mountain to prove how big you are, you almost never make it. And even if you do it's a hollow victory. In order to sustain the victory you have to prove yourself again and again in some other way, and again and again and again, driven forever to fill a false image, haunted by the fear that the image is not true and someone will find out."

> **False words are not only evil in themselves,**
> **but they infect the world with evil.**
>
> PLATO, in *Phaedo* (4th c. BC)

> **One of the penalties for refusing to participate in politics**
> **is that you end up being governed by your inferiors.**
>
> PLATO, in *The Republic* (4th c. BC)

> **There is simple ignorance,**
> **which is the source of lighter offenses,**
> **and double ignorance,**
> **which is accompanied by a conceit of wisdom;**
> **and he who is under the influence of the latter fancies that**
> **he knows all about matters of which he knows nothing.**
>
> PLATO, in *Laws, Book IX* (4th c. BC)

Without mentioning the author, I've now asked more than 100 people, "Which single person does this quotation describe best?" Regardless of political orientation, *all of them* answered in the same way.

The people have always some champion
whom they set over them and nurse into greatness...
This and no other is the root from which a tyrant springs;
when he first appears he is a protector.

PLATO, in *The Republic* (4th c. BC)

Of all the causes which conspire to blind
Man's erring judgment, and misguide the mind,
What the weak head with strongest bias rules
Is Pride, the never-failing vice of fools.

ALEXANDER POPE, in *An Essay on Criticism* (1711)

A man should never be ashamed
to own he has been in the wrong,
which is but saying, in other words,
that he is wiser today than he was yesterday.

ALEXANDER POPE, "Thoughts on Various
Subjects," in *Swift's Miscellanies* (1727)

Party is the madness of many, for the gain of the few.

ALEXANDER POPE, "Thoughts on Various
Subjects," in *Swift's Miscellanies* (1727)

It is with narrow-souled people
as with narrow-necked bottles;
The less they have in them the more
noise they make in pouring out.

ALEXANDER POPE, "Thoughts on Various
Subjects," in *Swift's Miscellanies* (1727)

An honest man's the noblest work of God.

ALEXANDER POPE, in *An Essay on Man* (1733)

The same ambition can destroy or save,
And makes a patriot as it makes a knave.
ALEXANDER POPE, in An Essay on Man (1733)

Ignorance is not a simple lack of knowledge
but an active aversion to knowledge, the refusal to know,
issuing from cowardice, pride, or laziness of mind.
KARL POPPER, as paraphrased by Ryszard Kapuscinski, in
The New York Times Magazine (Jan. 1, 1995)

Kapuscinski added: "In Popper's philosophy, ignorance has an ethical dimension, and knowing is a moral obligation for human beings."

None are fit judges of greatness
but those who are capable of it.
JANE PORTER, in Aphorisms of Sir Philip Sidney (1807)

For a politician to complain about the press
is like a ship's captain complaining about the sea.
ENOCH POWELL, quoted in The Guardian (Dec. 3, 1984)

The dangerous man is not the critic, but the noisy,
empty "patriot" who encourages us to
indulge in orgies of self-congratulation.
J. B. PRIESTLEY, in Rain Upon Godshill (1939)

Priestley introduced the thought by writing: "We should behave towards our country as women behave towards the men they love. A loving wife will do anything for her husband except to stop criticizing and trying to improve him. That is the right attitude for a citizen. We should cast the same affectionate but sharp glance at our country. We should love it, but also insist upon telling it all its faults."

**Those who wish
to appear wise
among fools,
among the wise
seem foolish.**

Quintilian

> In a fair gale every fool may sail,
> but wise behavior in a storm
> commends the wisdom of a pilot.
> FRANCIS QUARLES, in *Enchiridion* (1640)

> Look at [his] comments...
> They prove that the senator speaks his mind,
> and that he is not working with much when he does so.
> ANNA QUINDLEN, on Senator Jesse Helms,
> in *The New York Times* (June 13, 1993)

In my many conversations with Trump supporters, I've often heard them justify their support by saying, "I like him because he speaks his mind." For some reason, it never occurred to me to retort with a comment about the quality of the mind that was speaking. That changed after coming across Quindlen's terrific description of Sen. Helms.

In "The Longest Election Day," a Nov. 19, 2000 *Newsweek* article written in the middle of the hotly disputed Florida presidential election results, Anna Quindlen wrote:

> "We cannot always predict with certainty
> the future leader from the winning candidate.
> Some men grow in the job; others are diminished
> by its demands and its grandeur."

This is a wonderful observation, and would have become one of my 1,000 featured quotations if not for my decision to include only those written before the current century. Quindlen preceded her observation by writing: "An election marks the end of the affair...the seduction of the many by the few. Pretty words, fulsome promises. We wind up married, but to whom, to what?"

Those who wish to appear wise among fools,
among the wise seem foolish.

QUINTILIAN (MARCUS FABIUS QUINTILIANUS), in
De Institutione Oratoria (1st c. AD)

Quintilian's name may not be as familiar as Horace, Cicero, or Seneca, but to students of language, he is equally prominent. Not much is known about his personal life, but he founded the Roman Empire's most famous school of rhetoric. At age sixty, when most of his contemporaries were stepping away from an active and engaged life, he began the arduous task of publishing *De Institutione Oratoria*, a massive twelve-volume work on the theory and practice of oratory and rhetoric. His work was no ivory tower tome, though, and included many personal reflections on culture, education, human nature, morality, and other topics (a typical example was his well-known observation that ambition, while a vice, is the parent of many virtues).

De Institutione Oratoria went on to become enormously influential, especially among educated people who took their writing and speaking seriously. In his *Autobiography* (1873), John Stuart Mill wrote of Quintilian: "His book is a kind of encyclopedia of the thoughts of the ancients on the whole field of education and culture; and I have retained through life many valuable ideas which I can distinctly trace to my reading of him."

The observation above about those who appear wise to the foolish is the most famous Trump-related quotation from *De Institutione Oratoria*, but there are others as well:

A liar should have a good memory.

They condemn what they do not understand.

The prosperous cannot easily form a right idea of misery.

We must form our minds by reading deep rather than wide.

We should be moved ourselves
before we attempt to move others.

> There is no one who would not rather
> appear to know than to be taught.

Sayings designed to raise a laugh are
generally untrue and never complimentary.
Laughter is never far removed from derision.

> We should not speak so that it is possible
> for the audience to understand us,
> but so that it is impossible
> for them to misunderstand us.

**Never were abilities
so much
below mediocrity
so well rewarded.**

John Randolph

Do you know the hallmark of the second-rater?
It's resentment of another man's achievement.

AYN RAND, in *Atlas Shrugged* (1957)

The Argument from Intimidation
is a confession of intellectual impotence.

AYN RAND, in *The Virtue of Selfishness* (1964)

Rand introduced the thought by writing: "There is a certain type of argument which, in fact, is not an argument, but a means of forestalling debate and extorting an opponent's agreement with one's undiscussed notions. It is a message of bypassing logic by means of psychological pressure."

The self-confidence of a scientist
and the self-confidence of a con man
are not interchangeable states,
and do not come from the same psychological universe.
The success of a man who deals with reality
augments his self-confidence.
The success of a con man augments his panic.

AYN RAND, "The Comprachicos," in *The New Left* (1971)

Rationalization is a cover-up,
a process of providing one's emotions with a false identity,
of giving them spurious explanations and justifications—
in order to hide one's motives,
not just from others, put primarily from oneself.

AYN RAND, in *Philosophy: Who Needs It?* (1982)

Rand continued: "The price of rationalizing is the hampering, the distortion and, ultimately, the destruction of one's cognitive faculty.

Rationalization is a process of not perceiving reality, but of attempting to make reality fit one's emotions."

Never were abilities
so much below mediocrity
so well rewarded.

JOHN RANDOLPH, remark in US House of
Representatives (Feb. 1, 1828)

Congressman Randolph—often described in history books as simply "John Randolph of Roanoke"—was speaking about Benjamin Rush, who had recently been appointed Secretary of the Treasury by John Quincy Adams. Randolph's remark has long been considered the most scathing assessment of a presidential *appointment*, but there are many who now believe it can be applied to presidential elections as well.

Randolph, a man with a venomous wit, is responsible for another legendary political insult, this one directed at New York congressman Edward Livingston: "He is a man of splendid abilities, but utterly corrupt. He shines and stinks like rotten mackerel by moonlight."

Politics is supposed to be the second oldest profession.
I have come to realize that it bears
a very close resemblance to the first.

RONALD REAGAN, at a Los Angeles press conference (Mar. 2, 1977)

President Reagan was famous for "borrowing" lines from other sources and casually passing them off as his own. This one was likely inspired by a similar reference to politics and prostitution made by Canadian Prime Minister Lester B. Pearson in a 1967 speech to the Canadian Political Science Association: "I beg you not to despise the profession of politics. It's the second oldest in history, much more reputable even if less rewarding than the oldest."

People fed on sugared praises
cannot be expected to feel an appetite for
the black broth of honest criticism.
AGNES REPPLIER, in *Books and Men* (1888)

Give me a man or woman who has read a thousand books
and you give me an interesting companion.
Give me a man or woman who has read perhaps three
and you give me a very dangerous enemy indeed.
ANNE RICE, in *The Witching Hour* (1990)

Lying is done with words, and also with silence.
ADRIENNE RICH, in *On Lies, Secrets, and Silence* (1979)

This comes from Rich's essay "Women and Honor: Some Notes on Lying," which also contained these two additional thoughts on the subject:

"Lies are usually attempts to make
everything simpler—for the liar—
than it really is, or ought to be."

"The liar has many friends,
and leads an existence of great loneliness."

The personal pronoun "I" should be the
coat of arms of some individuals.
ANTOINE DE RIVAROL, quoted in M. M. Ballou,
Treasury of Thought (1872)

Politics is the science of domination,
and the persons in the process of
enlargement and illumination
are notoriously difficult to control.
Therefore, to protect its vested interests,
politics usurped religion a very long time ago.

TOM ROBBINS, in *Skinny Legs and All* (1990)

We are incredibly heedless in the formation of our beliefs,
but find ourselves filled with an illicit passion for them
when anyone proposes to rob us of their companionship.
It is obviously not the ideas themselves that are dear to us,
but our self-esteem, which is threatened.

JAMES HARVEY ROBINSON, in *The Mind in the Making* (1921)

Robinson introduced the thought by writing: "We sometimes find ourselves changing our minds without any resistance or heavy emotion, but if we are told that we are wrong we resent the imputation and harden our hearts."

We are all endowed with defense mechanisms
which operate automatically.
It is a poor technic [sic] when attempting to
convert one's neighbor to attack his beliefs directly,
especially those of the sacred variety.

JAMES HARVEY ROBINSON, in *The Human Comedy* (1937)

Robinson added: "We may flatter ourselves that we are undermining them by our potent reasoning only to find that we have shored them up so that they are firmer than ever."

> **The American people are a very generous people**
> **and will forgive almost any weakness,**
> **with the possible exception of stupidity.**
> WILL ROGERS, in *The Illiterate Digest* (1924)

In 1989, British member of parliament Roy Hattersley updated the idea when he was quoted in London's *Evening Standard* as saying: "In politics, being ridiculous is more damaging than being extreme."

> **When ignorance gets started, it knows no bounds.**
> WILL ROGERS, a 1926 remark, in *Will Rogers Speaks* (1995)

> **Politics is a busines where most of the men**
> **are looking for glory and personal gratification**
> **more than they do for money.**
> WILL ROGERS, a 1928 remark, in *Will Rogers Speaks* (1995)

> **Everything is changing in America.**
> **People are taking their comedians seriously**
> **and *the politicians as a joke,***
> **when it used to be vice versa.**
> WILL ROGERS, in "Will Rogers' Daily Telegram" (Nov. 22, 1932)

In his April 27, 2019 address at the White House Correspondents' Dinner, historian Ron Chernow got a big laugh from the audience when he offered a variation of this Will Rogers joke. Keynote speeches at this annual DC affair are typically delivered by comedians, not academics, but Chernow more than held his own, delivering what *The Guardian* newspaper called "an elegantly scathing rebuke" that mentioned Trump's name only once. The Rogers joke drew a big laugh, as did observations from other great wits. Perhaps the best line of the evening, though, was Chernow's own: "I applaud any president who aspires to the Nobel Prize for Peace, but we don't want one in the running for the Nobel Prize for Fiction."

> If we ever pass out as a great nation
> we ought to put on our tombstone
> "America died from a delusion that
> she had moral leadership."
>
> WILL ROGERS, quoted in Donald Day, *The Autobiography of Will Rogers* (1948)

> It is so much easier to be enthusiastic than to reason!
>
> ELEANOR ROOSEVELT, in *My Days* (1938)

> Those who attack always do so
> with greater fervor than those who defend.
>
> ELEANOR ROOSEVELT, in *My Days* (1938)

> Up to a certain point it is good for us to know
> that there are people in the world
> who will give us love and unquestioned
> loyalty to the limit of their ability.
> I doubt, however, if it is good for us
> to feel assured of this without
> the accompanying obligation of having to
> justify this devotion by our behavior.
>
> ELEANOR ROOSEVELT, in *The Autobiography of Eleanor Roosevelt* (1961)

The presidency is not merely
an administrative office. That's the least of it.
It is more than an engineering job, efficient or inefficient.
It is pre-eminently a place of moral leadership.

FRANKLIN D. ROOSEVELT, quoted in
The New York Times (Sep. 11, 1932)

Roosevelt said this in a speech shortly before his first presidential election victory. He continued: "All our great presidents were leaders of thought at times when certain historic ideas in the life of the nation had to be clarified." In the Trump Era, the idea that the American president is a "leader of thought" and his office "a place of moral leadership" is so ludicrous that it would be considered laughable were it not so tragic.

Repetition does not transform a lie into a truth.

FRANKLIN D. ROOSEVELT, in a "Fireside Chat"
radio address (Oct. 26, 1939)

We must especially beware
of that small group of selfish men
who would clip the wings of the American Eagle
in order to feather their own nests.

FRANKLIN D. ROOSEVELT, in his eighth State of
the Union Address (Jan. 6, 1941)

Bullies do not make brave men; and boys and men
of foul life cannot become good citizens,
good Americans, until they change; and
even after the change, scars will be left on their souls.

THEODORE ROOSEVELT, "The American Boy," in
St. Nicholas magazine (May 1900)

If a man continually blusters, if he lacks civility,
a big stick will not save him from trouble,

THEODORE ROOSEVELT, in address at
Minnesota State Fair (Sep. 2, 1901)

Roosevelt preceded this important thought about presidential demeanor with what most people would agree are his most famous words: "Speak softly and carry a big stick."

The man who makes a promise
which he does not intend to keep,
and does not try to keep, should rightly be adjudged
to have forfeited in some degree what should be
every man's most precious possession—his honor.

THEODORE ROOSEVELT, in speech in San
Francisco, CA (May 14, 1903)

We can as little afford to tolerate a dishonest man
in the public service as a coward in the army.

THEODORE ROOSEVELT, in a Washington, DC speech (Oct. 15, 1903)

This country has nothing to fear
from the crooked man who fails.
We put him in jail.
It is the crooked man who succeeds
who is a threat to this country.

THEODORE ROOSEVELT, in speech in Memphis,
Tennessee (Oct. 25, 1905)

If a man does not have an ideal and try to live up to it,
then he becomes a mean, base, and sordid creature,
no matter how successful.

THEODORE ROOSEVELT, in letter to his son Kermit (Jan. 27, 1915)

Unless a man is master of his soul,
all other kinds of mastery amount to little.

THEODORE ROOSEVELT, quoted in
Ladies' Home Journal (Jan. 1917)

To announce that there must be no criticism of the President,
or that we are to stand by the President, right or wrong,
is not only unpatriotic and servile,
but is morally treasonable to the American public.

THEODORE ROOSEVELT, in guest column in
The Kansas City Star (May 7, 1918)

The former president continued: "Nothing but the truth should be spoken about him or any one else. But it is even more important to tell the truth, pleasant or unpleasant, about him than about any one else."

Rationalizing is the very opposite of reasoning;
whereas reasoning works from evidence to conclusion,
rationalizing works from conclusion to evidence.
That is, rationalizing starts with what we *want* to be so
and then selectively compiles "evidence"
to prove that it *is* so.

VINCENT RYAN RUGGIERO, in *Beyond Feeling:
A Guide to Critical Thinking* (1995)

In general, pride is at the bottom of all great mistakes.

JOHN RUSKIN, in *Modern Painters* (1856)

The opinions that are held with passion
are always those for which no good ground exists;
indeed the passion is the measure
of the holder's lack of rational conviction.

BERTRAND RUSSELL, in *Sceptical Essays* (1928)

The megalomaniac differs from the narcissist by the fact
that he wishes to be powerful rather than charming,
and seeks to be feared rather than loved.
To this type belong many lunatics and
most of the great men of history.
BERTRAND RUSSELL, in *The Conquest of Happiness* (1930)

The fundamental cause of the trouble
is that in the modern world
the stupid are cocksure while the
intelligent are full of doubt.
BERTRAND RUSSELL, in "The Triumph of Stupidity" (1933)

A stupid man's report
of what a clever man says is never accurate,
because he unconsciously translates what he hears
into something that he can understand.
BERTRAND RUSSELL, in *A History of Western Philosophy* (1945)

You mustn't exaggerate, young man.
That's always a sign that your argument is weak.
BERTRAND RUSSELL, remark to Tommy Robbins,
in *Redbook* magazine (Sep. 1964)

**I did never know
so full a voice
issue from
so empty a heart.**
William Shakespeare

One of the saddest lessons of history is this:
If we've been bamboozled long enough,
we tend to reject any evidence of the bamboozle.
We're no longer interested in finding out the truth.
The bamboozle has captured us.
It's simply too painful to acknowledge,
even to ourselves, that we've been taken.

CARL SAGAN, in *The Demon-Haunted World* (1995)

We all run the risk of declining if somebody does not rise
to tell us that life is on the heights, and not in the cesspools.

GEORGE SAND, in letter to Charles Edmond (Jan. 9, 1858)

People lie because they can't help making a story
better than it was the way it happened.

CARL SANDBURG, in *The People, Yes* (1936)

Is it not true that the ability to apologize
is one of the elements of true greatness?
It is the small-souled man
who will not stoop to apologize.

J. OSWALD SANDERS, in *Christ Incomparable* (1953)

Those who cannot remember the past
are condemned to repeat it.

GEORGE SANTAYANA, in *The Life of Reason* (1905-1906)

This may be history's most famous saying on the importance of learning from the past. The essential proposition makes a lot of sense, of course, but throughout history individuals as well as nations have failed to heed the lesson. The problem has been described in a multitude of ways by a multitude of people. In his 1987 novel *Bluebeard*,

Kurt Vonnegut has a character express it well: "I've got news for Mr. Santayana: we're doomed to repeat the past no matter what. That's what it is to be alive."

Words are weapons, and it is dangerous in speculation,
as in politics, to borrow them from our enemies.
GEORGE SANTAYANA, in *Obiter Scripta* (1936)

If there has been a consistent phrase used by history's most resolute foes of freedom, it is, "The press is the enemy of the people," and to see President Trump repeating the words is one of the most shameful aspects of his presidency. If it is dangerous to borrow *words* from our enemies, it is even more destructive to borrow their *thoughts and ideas.* Who would've thought, for example, that an American president would embrace the following tactical observation from Joseph Goebbels: "Making noise is an effective means of opposition." Or behave in a way that is consistent with this thought from the author of *Mein Kampf*: "The art of leadership...consists in consolidating the attention of the people against a single adversary and taking care that nothing will split up that attention."

Our biggest problem as human beings
is not knowing that we don't know.
VIRGINIA SATIR, quoted in Jane Howard, *Please Touch* (1970)

True merit, like a river,
the deeper it is, the less noise it makes.
GEORGE SAVILE (Lord Halifax), in *Some Cautions Offered* (1699)

Against stupidity the gods
Themselves contend in vain.
JOHANN FRIEDRICH VON SCHILLER,
in *The Maid of Orleans* (1801)

Pride is an established conviction of
one's own paramount worth in some particular respect,
while *vanity* is the desire of rousing
such a conviction in others,
and it is generally accompanied by the secret hope
of ultimately coming to the same conviction oneself.
ARTHUR SCHOPENHAUER, in *Parerga and Paralipomena* (1851)

Schopenhauer continued: "Pride works *from within*; it is the direct appreciation of oneself. Vanity is the desire to arrive at this appreciation indirectly, *from without*."

It is a wise thing to be polite;
consequently, it is a stupid thing to be rude.
To make enemies by unnecessary and willful incivility
is just as insane a proceeding as to set your house on fire.
ARTHUR SCHOPENHAUER, in *Parerga and Paralipomena* (1851)

Men best show their character in trifles,
where they are not on their guard.
ARTHUR SCHOPENHAUER, in Tryon Edwards,
A Dictionary of Thoughts (1891)

Schopenhauer continued: "It is in insignificant matters, and in the simplest habits, that we often see the boundless egotism which pays no regard to the feeling of others, and denies nothing to itself."

Oh, what a tangled web we weave
When first we practice to deceive!

SIR WALTER SCOTT, in *Marmion* (1808)

If one doesn't know his mistakes,
he won't want to correct them.

LUCIUS ANNAEUS SENECA (Seneca the Younger),
in *Letters to Lucilius* (1st c. AD)

You can tell the character of every man
when you see how he gives and receives praise.

LUCIUS ANNAEUS SENECA (Seneca the Younger),
in *Letters to Lucilius* (1st c. AD)

It is not the man who has too little,
but the man who craves more, that is poor.

LUCIUS ANNAEUS SENECA (Seneca the Younger),
in *Letters to Lucilius* (1st c. AD)

To consort with the crowd is harmful;
there is no person who does not make
some vice attractive to us, or stamp it upon us,
or taint us unconsciously therewith.
Certainly, the greater the mob with which
we mingle, the greater the danger.

LUCIUS ANNAEUS SENECA (Seneca the Younger),
in *Letters to Lucilius* (1st c. AD)

The vulgar bark at men of mark,
as dogs bark at strangers.

LUCIUS ANNAEUS SENECA (Seneca the Younger), in
De Vita Beata [On the Happy Life] (1st c. AD)

... and the Wolf chewed up the children and spit out their bones ...
But those were <u>Foreign Children</u> and it really didn't matter."

Actual Dr. Seuss cartoon from 1941
criticizing America's policy on
denying European Jews safe-haven
during the Holocaust. Note the
slogan on the Mother's shirt.

> And the Wolf chewed
> up the children and
> spat out their bones...
> But they were
> *Foreign Children* and
> it really didn't matter.
>
> DR. SEUSS (Theodor Geisel),
> caption for cartoon in *PM
> Weekly* (Oct. 1, 1941)

Dr. Seuss (Theodor Geisel) did not become a household name until more than a decade after World War II ended (his breakthrough book was *The Cat in the Hat* in 1957). Few modern fans are aware of the important role Geisel played during World War II and in the years leading up to the conflict. A staunch foe of Fascism and Nazism, Geisel grew alarmed at an incipient "America First" movement that opposed US involvement in the growing European conflict, greatly minimized the threat posed by Hitler, and turned a cold shoulder to European Jews seeking refuge in the United States.

> And I have often heard it said unbidden guests
> Are often welcomest when they are gone.
>
> WILLIAM SHAKESPEARE, in *King Henry the Sixth, Part I* (1590)

This line from one of Shakespeare's earliest plays passes along a time-honored insight: people generally feel an enormous sense of relief when an unwelcome guest finally departs. For me, that day will arrive on January 20, 2021, when somebody new will be formally inaugurated as the nation's forty-sixth president.

This passage by Shakespeare reminded me of an observation from the fictional detective Adam Dalgliesh in *Death in Holy Orders*, a 2001 mystery novel by P. D. James. About another character, Dalgliesh says: "He was a man whose absence was usually preferable to his presence."

It's a wonderful line, and I have a strong intuition that Trump might be viewed in exactly this way by many of the people who've worked with him over the years. Think about it. In almost every family or social group, there's at least one person we can take in small doses, but who's difficult to be around for an extended period of time. These people are often "big-personality" types who, as the saying goes, suck up all the oxygen in a room. The reason these center-stagers wear thin, though, is because they also tend to be self-absorbed and opinionated people who love to talk (especially about themselves), and who rarely listen or show signs of genuine interest in other people. When such people leave a room after dominating it for a time, there is often a palpable feeling of relief experienced by those who remain (similar to the feeling generated by the departure of Shakespeare's "unbidden guests").

Small things make base men proud.
WILLIAM SHAKESPEARE, in *King Henry the Sixth, Part II* (1592)

He's sudden if a thing comes in his mind.
WILLIAM SHAKESPEARE, in *King Henry the Sixth, Part III* (1592)

If Shakespeare were writing today, I wouldn't be surprised to see him describe Trump as a "sudden talker," meaning someone who says things as soon as they come to his mind, without pausing to reflect on their meaning, relevance, or appropriateness.

> **When the lion fawns upon the lamb,**
> **The lamb will never cease to follow him.**
> WILLIAM SHAKESPEARE, in *King Henry the Sixth, Part III* (1592)

> **Sweet mercy is nobility's true badge.**
> WILLIAM SHAKESPEARE, in *Titus Andronicus* (1593-1594)

Here, the character Tamora is giving advice to the title character, a Roman general who has just become Emperor. She preceded the thought by saying: "Wilt thou draw near the nature of the gods? Draw near them then in being merciful."

> **The devil can cite Scripture for his purpose.**
> **An evil soul producing holy witness**
> **Is like a villain with a smiling cheek,**
> **A goodly apple rotten at the heart.**
> **O, what a goodly outside falsehood hath.**
> WILLIAM SHAKESPEARE, in *The Merchant of Venice* (1596)

> **Let none presume**
> **To wear an undeserved dignity.**
> WILLIAM SHAKESPEARE, in *The Merchant of Venice* (1596)

The words come from the Prince of Aragon, who is arguing that high standing should be based on merit rather than achieved through corrupt or ignoble means. He continued:

"O that estates, degrees, and offices,
Were not derived corruptly, and that clear honor
Were purchased by the merit of the wearer."

There's not one wise man among twenty will praise himself.
WILLIAM SHAKESPEARE, in *Much Ado About Nothing* (1598)

Happy are they that hear their detractions
and can put them to mending.
WILLIAM SHAKESPEARE, in *Much Ado About Nothing* (1598)

The fool doth think he is wise,
but the wise man knows himself to be a fool.
WILLIAM SHAKESPEARE, in *As You Like It* (1599)

Such men as he be never at heart's ease
Whiles they behold a greater than themselves,
And therefore are they very dangerous.
WILLIAM SHAKESPEARE, in *Julius Caesar* (1599)

I did never know so full a voice
issue from so empty a heart:
but the saying is true,
"The empty vessel makes the greatest sound."
WILLIAM SHAKESPEARE, in *King Henry V* (1599)

As a lifelong quotation collector, this was one of the most exciting discoveries in my recent research efforts. The words come from a minor character (known only as "Boy"), who is describing Pistol, a recurring Shakespeare character. Pistol is a swaggering soldier who attempts to hide his cowardice behind bloviations about his great prowess. The *full voice/empty heart* phrase above is a neat bit of verbal styling, but few quotation lovers are familiar with it, for *all* editions of *Bartlett's Familiar Quotations,* from the first in 1855 to the eighteenth in 2012, have presented the passage in the following way:

> "But the saying is true,
> 'The empty vessel makes the greatest sound.'"

Why John Bartlett and all of the subsequent *Bartlett's* editors for almost 150 years would choose to omit the wonderful opening line is a mystery. But I'm happy to rectify that error—and to also suggest the phrase as an apt description of Donald Trump.

I set it down
That one may smile, and smile, and be a villain.
WILLIAM SHAKESPEARE, in *Hamlet* (1601)

Assume a virtue, if you have it not.
WILLIAM SHAKESPEARE, in *Hamlet* (1601)

Madness in great ones must not unwatched go.
WILLIAM SHAKESPEARE, in *Hamlet* (1601)

There is no darkness but ignorance.
WILLIAM SHAKESPEARE, in *Twelfth Night* (1601)

Who knows himself a braggart,
Let him fear this: for it will come to pass,
That every braggart shall be found an ass.
WILLIAM SHAKESPEARE, in *All's Well That Ends Well* (1604)

Oft expectation fails, and most oft there
where most it promises.
WILLIAM SHAKESPEARE, in *All's Well That Ends Well* (1604)

To have what we would have,
we speak not what we mean.
WILLIAM SHAKESPEARE, in *Measure for Measure* (1604)

The miserable have no other medicine
But only hope.
WILLIAM SHAKESPEARE, in *Measure for Measure* (1604)

What a sweep of vanity comes this way.
WILLIAM SHAKESPEARE, in *Timon of Athens* (c. 1607)

This is a minor character's remark at the sight of an approaching group of women, all dressed in Amazon costumes, dancing, and playing lutes. The *sweep of vanity* saying has not yet been used by any of Trump's critics or political opponents, but it's such a delicious phrase that I expect it will soon be showing up on the campaign trail.

There is no more mercy in him
than there is in a male tiger.
WILLIAM SHAKESPEARE, in *Coriolanus* (1607–08)

His garments are rich,
but he wears them not handsomely.
WILLIAM SHAKESPEARE, in *The Winter's Tale* (1610–1611)

Heat not a furnace for your foe so hot
That it do singe yourself.

WILLIAM SHAKESPEARE, in *Henry VIII* (1613)

He knows nothing; and he thinks he knows everything.
That points clearly to a political career.

GEORGE BERNARD SHAW, in *Major Barbara* (1905)

When we think of cruelty,
we must try to remember
the stupidity, the envy, the frustration
from which it has arisen.

EDITH SITWELL, in *Taken Care Of* (1965)

The aim of flattery is to soothe and encourage us
by assuring us of the truth of an opinion
we have already formed about ourselves.

EDITH SITWELL, in E. Salter, *The Last Years of a Rebel* (1967)

I am patient with stupidity,
but not with those who are proud of it.

EDITH SITWELL, in E. Salter, *The Last Years of a Rebel* (1967)

Arrogance is grasping for *power*
that we fear we don't deserve.
It is more serious than boasting,
which is only a grab for praise,
covering for what we suspect is empty inside.

LEWIS B. SMEDES, in *Love Within Limits* (1978)

A bit later, Smedes added: "Because arrogance is born in personal vanity, arrogant people are driven without mercy. They can never get enough power to fill the soul's needs or enough respect to overcome the fear that they deserve less than they are getting."

Rudeness should not be confused with crudeness.
The crude person is one who has not
learned the manners of society.
The rude person is the one who is so
hell-bent on staying upright
that in his anxiety he cuts and bruises
anyone who threatens him,
even as he uses anyone who can help him.

LEWIS B. SMEDES, in *Love Within Limits* (1978)

Smedes continued: "Rudeness, too, comes from emptiness. The poised person, by contrast, can quietly fit in any time or place without having to call attention to himself. He does not have to *look* strong by bullying the servants or manipulating the powerful."

They are the most frivolous
and superficial of mankind only
who can be much delighted with that praise
which they themselves know to be altogether unmerited.

ADAM SMITH, in *The Theory of Moral Sentiments* (1759)

Everything that deceives may be said to enchant.

SOCRATES, quoted by Plato in *The Republic* (4th c. BC)

Are you not ashamed that you
give your attention to acquiring as much money as possible,
and similarly with reputation and honor,
and give no attention or thought to truth and understanding
and the perfection of your soul?
SOCRATES, quoted by Plato in *Apology* (4th c. BC)

How can you expect a man who's warm
to understand one who's cold?
ALEXANDER SOLZHENITSYN, in *One Day in
the Life of Ivan Denisovich* (1962)

It is not because the truth is too difficult to see
that we make mistakes. It may even lie on the surface;
but we make mistakes because the easiest
and most comfortable course for us is to seek insight
where it accords with our emotions—especially selfish ones.
ALEXANDER SOLZHENITSYN, in *Solzhenitsyn:
A Documentary Record* (1974)

Shouting has never made me understand anything.
SUSAN SONTAG, in *The Benefactor* (1963)

What is morally wrong cannot be politically right.
DONALD SOPER, in a 1966 House of Lords speech

Beware of anyone who answers your question
before you have finished it.
THOMAS SOWELL, "Random Thoughts," in
Barbarians Inside the Gates (1999)

People who answer questions before they're fully posed don't regard what they're having as a *conversation* so much as a verbal sparring contest. If such people were to wait patiently until questions are completely formulated, they'd be ceding an advantage. In Trump's zero-sum world of winners and losers, that will simply not do.

In the John Locke entry earlier, interrupting was described as a form of rudeness. In Trump's case, though, it is not so much related to insensitivity as it is to the desire to gain an interpersonal advantage. We've seen it demonstrated countless times, but never more dramatically than in the Fox News Republican Primary Debate on Aug. 6, 2015.

Moderator Megan Kelly opened the debate with a question directed to Trump: "You've called women you don't like 'fat pigs,' 'dogs,' 'slobs,' and 'disgusting animals'…" When Trump interrupted to say, "Only Rosie O'Donnell," there was some laughter and hoots from the audience. Kelly went on to finish her question, and Trump gave a forgettable answer that involved something about political correctness.

When "Dilbert" author Scott Adams analyzed the moment in *Win Bigly* (2017), he said that Kelly's question "should have ended his campaign on the spot. Only a few people in the world could have escaped her trap." But after Trump's interruption, Adams wrote:

> "By then it didn't matter. The Rosie O'Donnell reference sucked all the energy out of the room. It was a masterstroke of persuasion, timed perfectly, and executed in front of the world. When I saw it happen, I stood and walked toward the television (literally). I got goose bumps on my arm. *This wasn't normal.* This was persuasion like I have never seen it performed in public. And in that moment, I saw the future unfold."

**There are too many people
who ought to be grateful for their good fortune,
but who are arrogant instead.**

THOMAS SOWELL, "Random Thoughts," in
Barbarians Inside the Gates (1999)

Sowell has been a leading figure in conservative/libertarian thought for many decades. While we differ in a number of key ways, I have long admired his graceful and elegant way with words. Many of his observations, like the one above about good fortune leading to arrogance rather than gratefulness, seem as if they could've been written specifically about Donald Trump. Here some others that also seem to apply:

**Politics is the art of finding clever
reasons for doing dumb things.**

**Some people are such masters of the half-truth
that it would be a waste of talent for them to lie.**

**It is amazing how much time and ingenuity
people will put into defending some idea
that they never bothered to
think through in the first place.**

**When you want to help people,
you tell them the truth.
When you want to help yourself,
you tell them what they want to hear.**

**It always amazes me how many people there are
who never seem to understand that what they have done
has contributed to the consequences that followed.**

**One of the most pathetic—and dangerous—signs
of our times is the growing number of individuals
and groups who believe that no one can possibly
disagree with them for any honest reason.**

People who believe in conspiracy theories
should ask themselves:
Have you ever tried to keep a secret among five people?
Even Mafia dons get squealed on.

Maturity is not a matter of age.
You have matured when you are no longer
concerned with showing how clever you are,
and give your full attention to getting the job done right.
Many never reach that stage, no matter how old they get.

What a cage is to the wild beast,
law is to the selfish man.
HERBERT SPENCER, in *Social Statics* (1850)

This quotation came to my attention in the summer of 2016 when candidate Trump made repeated assertions that US District Judge Gonzalo P. Curiel could not be impartial in the upcoming class action lawsuit against Trump University. Trump repeatedly described the judge as "a Mexican," even though he was born in Indiana. It was shameful behavior, and it was described perfectly by Herbert Spencer 165 years earlier. Even the *Wall Street Journal,* not the most critical organ when it comes to Trump, called his remarks "truly odious."

Trump's actions in the Trump University lawsuit mirrored his behavior in every legal predicament he's ever been in. He rattles the cage like a wild beast, attacking the law, the evidence, the prosecutors or plaintiffs, the witnesses, and even the judge.

Imagine for a moment how candidate Trump would have handled a loss in the 2016 presidential election. The charges of "a rigged system," "voter fraud," "mystery ballots," "voting by illegal aliens," and more would still be ringing in our ears. This is a man who is psychologically unable to take a defeat lightly—or gracefully. Think about his likely response if he loses the 2020 presidential election in a squeaker. The prospect is almost too painful to consider—and such a troubling scenario can only be avoided if he is so resoundingly trounced that he has no other recourse but to accept defeat.

How often misused words
generate misleading thoughts.
HERBERT SPENCER, in *The Principles of Ethics* (1879)

The bigger the brag, the poorer the feat.
C. H. SPURGEON, in *The Salt-Cellars* (1889)

Our own self-love draws a thick veil
between us and our faults.
PHILIP DORMER STANHOPE (Lord Chesterfield),
in letter to his son (June 21, 1748)

People hate those who
make them feel their own inferiority.
PHILIP DORMER STANHOPE (Lord Chesterfield),
in letter to his son (Apr. 30, 1750)

Every man can be cunning if he pleases,
by simulation, dissimulation, and in short by lying.
But that character is universally despised
and detested, and justly too;
no truly great man was ever cunning.
PHILIP DORMER STANHOPE (Lord Chesterfield), in *Letters
from a Celebrated Nobleman to His Heir* (1783)

Among all the diseases of the mind
there is not one more epidemical
or more pernicious than the love of flattery.
RICHARD STEELE, in *The Spectator* (Dec. 3, 1711)

You can boast about anything if it's all you have.
Maybe the less you have, the more you are required to boast.
JOHN STEINBECK, in *East of Eden* (1952)

Trust that man in nothing
who has not a conscience in everything.
LAURENCE STERNE, in *Tristram Shandy* (1759–1767)

The cruelest lies are often told in silence.
ROBERT LOUIS STEVENSON, in *Virginibus Puerisque* (1881)

A few years later, Amelia E. Barr made a similar point when she wrote
about a character in *The Bow of Orange Ribbon* (1886): "She had not spoken false words, but truth can be outraged by silence quite as cruelly
as by speech."

Politics is perhaps the only profession
for which no preparation is thought necessary.
ROBERT LOUIS STEVENSON, in *Familiar
Studies of Men and Books* (1882)

To assert dignity is to lose it.
REX STOUT, Nero Wolfe speaking, in *The
League of Frightened Men* (1935)

When political ammunition runs low,
inevitably the rusty artillery of abuse is wheeled into action.

WALLACE STEVENS, in a New York City speech (Sep. 22, 1952)

[He] had tall tales to tell,
but that is not uncommon among inferior men.
He was only one of a long series of males,
who for one reason or another, to boost their own ego,
find it satisfying to boast of what they have not achieved.

HAN SUYIN, in *A Mortal Flower* (1965)

Falsehood flies, and the truth comes limping after it.

JONATHAN SWIFT, in *The Examiner* (Nov. 2, 1710)

According to quotation researchers, this is the earliest appearance of a sentiment that ultimately morphed into an anonymously authored saying that is often mistakenly attributed to Mark Twain: "A lie can travel around the world and back again while the truth is lacing up its boots." The fuller passage from Swift's essay is as follows:

"Besides, as the vilest writer has his readers, so the greatest liar has his believers; and it often happens, that if a lie be believ'd only for an hour, it has done its work, and there is no farther [sic] occasion for it. Falsehood flies, and the truth comes limping after it; so that when men come to be undeceiv'd, it is too late; the jest is over, and the tale has had its effect."

We have just Religion enough to make us *hate*,
but not enough to make us *love* one another.

JONATHAN SWIFT, in *Thoughts on Various Subjects* (1711)

I never wonder to see men wicked,
but I often wonder to see them not ashamed.

JONATHAN SWIFT, in *Thoughts on Various Subjects* (1711)

Nothing is so hard for those, who abound in riches,
as to conceive how others can be in want.

JONATHAN SWIFT, "A Preface to the Bishop of
Sarum's Introduction" (Dec. 8, 1713)

Reasoning will never make a man correct an ill opinion,
which by reasoning he never acquired.

JONATHAN SWIFT, in *Letter to a Young Clergyman* (1720)

How haughtily he cocks his nose,
To tell what every schoolboy knows.

JONATHAN SWIFT, on a contemporary, in 1722 poem

You can see current events in their
historical perspective, provided that your
passion for the truth prevails over your bias.

LEO SZILARD, "Are We on the Road to War?" in
Bulletin of the Atomic Scientists (Apr. 1962)

Not all readers
become leaders.
But all leaders
must be readers.

Harry S Truman

The weak can be terrible
because they try furiously to be strong.
RABINDRANATH TAGORE, in *Fireflies* (1928)

Blind and naked Ignorance
Delivers brawling judgments, unashamed,
On all things all day long.
ALFRED, LORD TENNYSON, in *Idylls of the King* (1859-1885)

Riches, both material and spiritual,
can choke you if you do not use them fairly.
MOTHER TERESA, in *No Greater Love* (1997)

Mother Teresa went on to add: "One day there springs up the desire
for money and for all that money can provide—the superfluous, luxury in eating, luxury in dressing, trifles. Needs increase because one
thing calls for another. The result is uncontrollable dissatisfaction."

Politics is a game of compromise...faith isn't.
CAL THOMAS, a 1985 remark in *Newsweek* (Nov. 12, 2006)

Such as every man is inwardly, so he judgeth outwardly.
THOMAS À KEMPIS, in *Imitation of Christ* (c. 1420)

He is truly great that is great in charity.
He is truly great that is little in himself,
and that maketh no account of any height of honors.
THOMAS À KEMPIS, in *Imitation of Christ* (c. 1420)

Base envy withers at another's joy,
And hates that excellence it cannot reach.

JAMES THOMSON, in the poem "Spring" (1728)

One man lies in his words, and gets a bad reputation;
another in his manners, and enjoys a good one.

HENRY DAVID THOREAU, journal entry (June 25, 1851)

One of the definitions of sanity, itself,
is the ability to tell real from unreal.
Shall we need a new definition?

ALVIN TOFFLER, in *Future Shock* (1970)

There is no greatness where there is not
simplicity, goodness, and truth.

LEO TOLSTOY, in *War and Peace* (1860)

The constant, obvious flattery, contrary to all evidence,
of the people around him had brought him to the point
that he no longer saw his contradictions, no longer
conformed his actions and words to reality, logic, or
even simple common sense, but was fully convinced
that all his orders, however senseless, unjust, and
inconsistent with each other, became sensible, just, and
consistent with each other only because he gave them.

LEO TOLSTOY, the narrator describing
Tsar Nicholas I, in *Hadji Murad* (1912)

A bit earlier in the novel, after the tsar received some flattering remarks
from an aide, the narrator described his reaction this way: "This praise
of his strategic abilities was especially pleasing to Nicholas, because,
though he was proud of his strategic abilities, at the bottom of his

heart he was aware that he had none. And now he wanted to hear more detailed praise of himself." For more on this passage, see my discussion of it in the Introduction.

True leadership must be for the benefit of the followers,
not the enrichment of the leaders.
ROBERT TOWNSEND, in *Further Up the Organization* (1984)

If the citizens of the United States were indeed
the devoted patriots they call themselves,
they would surely not thus encrust themselves
in the hard, dry, stubborn persuasion
that they are the first and best of the human race,
that nothing is to be learnt,
but what they are able to teach,
and that nothing is worth having,
which they do not possess.
FRANCES TROLLOPE, in *Domestic Manners of the Americans* (1832)

In reading the lives of great men,
I found that the first victory they won
was over themselves and their carnal urges.
Self-discipline with all of them came first.
HARRY S TRUMAN, in *The Autobiography of Harry S Truman* (1980)

Not all readers become leaders.
But all leaders must be readers.
HARRY S TRUMAN, quoted in M. M. Poen, *Strictly Personal and Confidential—The Letters Harry Truman Never Mailed* (1982)

In 1962, historian Barbara Tuchman came out with *The Guns of August*, a detailed account of the first month of World War I (it went on to win the Pulitzer Prize for General Non-Fiction). The book so impressed President John F. Kennedy that he invited Tuchman to the White House. He also made her book required reading for his top aides, leading Theodore Sorenson to remark: "He made sure that all of us working with him had read that book and understood his concern." I don't believe there is a single person in the entire world—even counting Trump's most fervent supporters—who can imagine a similar scenario occurring in the Trump White House.

Honor wears different coats to different eyes.
BARBARA W. TUCHMAN, in *The Guns of August* (1962)

**Strong prejudices in an ill-formed mind
are hazardous to government, and when
combined with a position of power even more so.**
BARBARA W. TUCHMAN, in *The March of Folly* (1984)

**Government remains the paramount area of folly
because it is there that men seek power over others—
only to lose it over themselves.**
BARBARA W. TUCHMAN, in *The March of Folly* (1984)

You can't pray a lie.
MARK TWAIN, the title character speaking, in
The Adventures of Huckleberry Finn (1885)

**All you need in this life is ignorance and confidence,
and then success is sure.**
MARK TWAIN, in letter to Mrs. Foote (Dec. 2, 1887)

When the doctrine of allegiance to party
can utterly up-end a man's moral constitution
and make a temporary fool of him besides,
what excuse are you going to offer for preaching it,
teaching it, extending it, perpetuating it?

MARK TWAIN, in an 1887 speech in Hartford, CT

Twain continued: "Shall you say, the best good of the country demands allegiance to party? Shall you also say it demands that a man kick his truth and his conscience into the gutter, and become a mouthing lunatic, besides?"

My kind of loyalty was loyalty to one's country,
not to its institutions or its office-holders.

MARK TWAIN, in *A Connecticut Yankee in King Arthur's Court* (1889)

These words come from Hank Morgan, the narrator and protagonist of the novel. He continued: "The country is the real thing, the substantial thing, the eternal thing; it is the thing to watch over, and care for, and be loyal to; institutions are extraneous, they are its mere clothing, and clothing can wear out, become ragged, cease to be comfortable, cease to protect the body from winter, disease, and death. To be loyal to rags, to shout for rags, to worship rags, to die for rags—that is a loyalty of unreason."

Noise proves nothing.
Often a hen who has merely laid an egg
cackles as if she had laid an asteroid.

MARK TWAIN, in *Following the Equator* (1897)

We do not deal much in fact
when we are contemplating ourselves.

MARK TWAIN, "Does the Race of Man Love a Lord?" in
The North American Review (Apr. 1902)

I am quite sure now that often, very often,
in matters concerning religion and politics
a man's reasoning powers are not above the monkey's.

MARK TWAIN, an autobiographical dictation (Sep. 12, 1907)

In religion and politics people's beliefs and convictions
are in almost every case gotten at second hand,
and without examination, from authorities who have
not themselves examined the questions at issue but have
taken them at second-hand from other non-examiners.

MARK TWAIN, *an autobiographical dictation* (July 10, 1908)

It is curious—curious that physical courage should be
so common in the world, and moral courage so rare.

MARK TWAIN, quoted in Bernard DeVoto,
Mark Twain in Eruption (1940)

**The voters
are the people
who have spoken—
the bastards.**

Morris K. Udall

The voters are the people
who have spoken—the bastards.
MORRIS K. UDALL, in the *Chicago Sun-Times* (July 14, 1976)

What we believe to be the motives of our conduct
are usually but the pretexts for it.
MIGUEL DE UNAMUNO, in *The Tragic Sense of Life* (1912)

All fires burn out at last.
SIGRID UNDSET, in *Kristin Lavransdatter: The Cross* (1922)

Americans have been conditioned to respect newness,
whatever it costs them.
JOHN UPDIKE, in *A Month of Sundays* (1975)

Government is either
organized benevolence or organized madness;
its peculiar magnitude permits no shading.
JOHN UPDIKE, in *Buchanan Dying* (1974)

All you have the right to ask of life
is to choose a battle in this war,
make the best you can,
and leave the field with honor.
LEON URIS, in *Mila 18* (1961)

I was brought up not only to develop the spirit of tolerance
but also to cherish moral and spiritual qualities
such as modesty, humility, compassion, and, most important,
to attain a certain degree of emotional equilibrium.
U THANT, in *View from the UN* (1978)

**Anyone who has the power
to make you believe absurdities
has the power to
make you commit injustices.**

Voltaire

An attitude of permanent indignation
signifies great mental poverty.
PAUL VALÉRY, in *Tel Quel* (1943)

Valéry continued: "Politics compels its votaries to take that line and
you can see their minds growing more and more impoverished every
day, from one burst of righteous anger to the next."

It is almost impossible to throw dirt on someone
without getting a little on yourself.
ABIGAIL VAN BUREN, in a 1991 "Dear Abby" column

Human beings are perhaps never more frightening than
when they are convinced beyond doubt that they are right.
LAURENS VAN DER POST, in *The Last World of the Kalahari* (1958)

Organized religion is making Christianity political
rather than making politics Christian.
LAUREN VAN DER POST, quoted in *The Observer* (Nov. 9, 1986)

On the throne of the world,
any delusion can become fact.
GORE VIDAL, in *Julian: A Novel* (1964)

Unless drastic reforms are made,
we must accept the fact that every four years
the United States will be up for sale,
and the richest man or family will buy it.
GORE VIDAL, in *Reflections Upon a Sinking Ship* (1969)

Vidal preceded the thought by writing: "I think it is tragic that the poor man has almost no chance to rise unless he is willing to put himself in thrall to moneyed interests."

> **Persuading the people to vote against
> their own best interests
> has been the awesome genius
> of the American political elite from the beginning.**
> GORE VIDAL, in *New York Review of Books* (Aug. 10, 1972)

In *The Decline and Fall of the American Empire* (1992), Vidal returned to the theme: "As societies grow decadent, the language grows decadent, too. Words are used to disguise, not to illuminate... Words are to confuse, so that at election time people will solemnly vote against their own interests."

> **That peculiarly American religion, President-worship.**
> GORE VIDAL, "President and Mrs. Grant" (1975);
> in *Matters of Fact and Fiction* (1978)

> **Religions are manipulated in order to serve those
> who govern society and not the other way around.**
> GORE VIDAL, "Sex Is Politics" (1979); in *The
> Second American Revolution* (1983)

> **Half the American people never read a newspaper.
> Half never vote for President—the same half?**
> GORE VIDAL, in *Screening History* (1992)

> **It is dangerous to be right in matters
> where established authorities are wrong.**
> VOLTAIRE, in *The Age of Louis XIV* (1751)

Every man is guilty of all the good he didn't do.
VOLTAIRE, in *The Age of Louis XIV* (1751)

Eleanor Roosevelt may have been thinking about this famous Voltaire observation when she wrote in *Tomorrow is Now* (1963): "What you don't do can be a destructive force."

While loving glory so much,
how can you persist in a plan which
will cause you to lose it?
VOLTAIRE, in letter to Frederick the Great (Oct. 1757)

He who thinks himself wise, O heavens! is a great fool.
VOLTAIRE, in *Le Droit du Seigneur* (written 1762,
first performed posthumously in 1779)

Prejudices are what fools use for reason.
VOLTAIRE, in *Philosophical Dictionary* (1764)

Anyone who has the power to make you believe absurdities
has the power to make you commit injustices.
VOLTAIRE, in *Questions on Miracles* (1765)

Voltaire offered many profound thoughts in his lifetime, and few can rival these powerful words. He continued: "If you do not use the intelligence with which God endowed your mind to resist believing impossibilities, you will not be able to use the sense of injustice which God planted in your heart to resist a command to do evil. Once a single faculty of your soul has been tyrannized, all the other faculties will submit to the same fate."

It is difficult to free fools from the chains they revere.

VOLTAIRE, in *The Dinner of Count Boulainvilliers* (1767)

I have never made but one prayer to God,
a very short one:
"O Lord, make my enemies ridiculous."
And God granted it.

VOLTAIRE, in letter to Étienne Damilaville (May 16, 1767)

We are what we pretend to be,
so we must be careful about what we pretend to be.

KURT VONNEGUT, in Introduction to *Mother Night* (1962)

Where's evil? It's that large part
of every man that wants to hate without limit,
that wants to hate with God on its side.
It's that part of every man that finds
all kinds of ugliness so attractive.

KURT VONNEGUT, in *Mother Night* (1962)

I believe that reading and writing are the most nourishing
forms of meditation anyone has so far found.
By reading the writings of the most
interesting minds in history, we meditate
with our own minds and theirs as well.
This to me is a miracle.

KURT VONNEGUT, in speech at dedication of the Shain Library,
Connecticut College, New London, CT (Oct. 1, 1976)

**Guard against
the impostures of
pretended patriotism.**

George Washington

> People do not wish to appear foolish;
> to avoid the appearance of foolishness,
> they were willing to remain actually fools.
>
> ALICE WALKER, in *In Search of Our Mothers' Gardens* (1983)

This quotation came to mind numerous times over the past several years, but never more bizarrely than in March 2019 when Devin Nunes, a Republican congressman from California filed a $250 million defamation lawsuit against Twitter and a number of named Twitter users (he was also seeking $350 million in punitive damages). The accounts named in the suit included "Devin Nunes' Cow" (@DevinCow), a parody account that employed bovine-related puns to poke fun at the congressman.

The puns that the thin-skinned Nunes found so damaging included one that mockingly described him as "udder-ly worthless" and another that referred to him as "a treasonous cowpoke." On the day Nunez filed his lawsuit, @DevinCow had 1,200 followers. Within days of the lawsuit, that number had skyrocketed to well over 600,000, far surpassing the number of Nunes's own Twitter followers.

> People always overdo the matter
> when they attempt deception.
>
> CHARLES DUDLEY WARNER, in *My Summer in a Garden* (1871)

> I prefer a man who will burn the flag
> and then wrap himself in the Constitution
> to a man who will burn the Constitution
> and then wrap himself in the flag.
>
> CRAIG WASHINGTON, a Texas state representative, quoted by
> Molly Ivins in *The Fort Worth Star-Telegram* (June 29, 1997)

Always submit your judgment to others with modesty.
GEORGE WASHINGTON, a "Rule of Civility" that guided his life

Sometime before his sixteenth birthday, Virginia schoolboy George Washington completed a penmanship exercise in which he hand copied a list of 110 "Rules of Civility & Decent Behavior in Company and Conversation." The list was originally prepared by French Jesuits around 1595 and first published in English in 1640. The Rules, which became popular in the education of young European aristocrats, found their way to America in the early 1700s. Technically, the words come from "Author Unknown," but it is because of Washington that we remember them today. Some of the other Rules of Civility that seem relevant in any discussion of Donald Trump are as follows:

Be not apt to relate news
if you know not the truth thereof.

> Show not yourself glad at the misfortune
> of another though he were your enemy.

Labor to keep alive in your breast that
little spark of celestial fire called conscience.

> Speak not injurious words neither in jest nor earnest;
> scoff at none although they give occasion.

Associate yourself with men of good quality
if you esteem your own reputation;
for 'tis better to be alone than in bad company

> Reprehend not the imperfections of others.

Be not tedious in discourse, make not many digressions.

> Utter not base and frivolous things
> amongst grave and learned men.

In disputes, be not so desirous to overcome as not
to give liberty to each one to deliver his opinion.

Example, whether it be good or bad,
has a powerful influence.
GEORGE WASHINGTON, in letter to Lord Stirling (Mar. 5, 1780)

We ought not to deceive ourselves.
GEORGE WASHINGTON, in letter to Joseph Reed (May 28, 1780)

Integrity and firmness of purpose are all I can promise.
These, be the voyage long or short, shall never forsake me.
GEORGE WASHINGTON, in letter to Henry Knox (Apr. 1, 1789),
a month before his inauguration as the first US president

There is but one straight course,
and that is to seek truth and pursue it steadily.
GEORGE WASHINGTON, in letter to Edmund Randolph (July 31, 1795)

Moderate the fury of party spirit.
GEORGE WASHINGTON, in his Farewell Address (Sep. 17, 1796)

Guard against the impostures of pretended patriotism.
GEORGE WASHINGTON, in his Farewell Address (Sep. 17, 1796)

In his address to the American people, the retiring president offered
this as one of a number of "counsels of an old and affectionate friend."
Washington's advice came to mind scores of times during Trump's

presidency, but it hit me most powerfully when he walked onstage at the CPAC (Conservative Political Action Committee) convention on February 15, 2019 and literally embraced the flag—to the wild cheers of adoring fans.

> To speak evil of anyone,
> unless there is unequivocal proofs of their deserving it,
> is an injury for which there is no adequate reparation.
>
> GEORGE WASHINGTON, in letter to George
> Washington Parke Custis (Nov. 28, 1796)

> Falsehoods not only disagree with truths,
> but usually quarrel among themselves.
>
> DANIEL WEBSTER, remark to jury in Salem, Mass. trial (Aug. 1830)

Webster said this to the jury in the 1830 trial of John Knapp for murdering Captain Joseph White. This is how the observation is commonly presented, but it was originally the conclusion of this larger thought: "Truth always fits. Truth is always congruous, and agrees with itself; every truth in the universe agrees with every other truth in the universe, whereas falsehoods not only disagree with truths, but usually quarrel among themselves."

> There is no nation on earth powerful
> enough to accomplish our overthrow.
> Our destruction, should it come at all,
> will be from another quarter.
> From the inattention of the people
> to the concerns of their government,
> from their carelessness and negligence.
>
> DANIEL WEBSTER, address in Madison, Indiana (June 1, 1837)

Webster continued: "I must confess that I do apprehend some danger. I fear that *they may place too implicit a confidence in their public servants and fail properly to scrutinize their conduct* [italics mine]; that in this way they may be made *the dupes of designing men and become the instruments of their own undoing* [italics mine]."

When a citizen gives his suffrage
to a man of known immorality, he abuses his trust;
he sacrifices not only his own interest,
but that of his neighbor;
he betrays the interest of his country.

NOAH WEBSTER, in *Letters to a Young Man*
Commencing His Education (1823)

All sins are attempts to fill voids.

SIMONE WEIL, in *Gravity and Grace* (1947)

The love of our neighbor in all its fullness
simply means being able to say to him:
"What are you going through?"

SIMONE WEIL, in *Waiting for God* (1950)

An individual's arrogance is always
in proportion to his lack of self-assurance.

OTTO WEININGER, in *Sex and Character* (1903)

I mistrust the judgment of every man
in a case in which his own wishes are concerned.

ARTHUR WELLESLEY (First Duke of Wellington), in
letter to Major Shawe (Feb. 3, 1805)

Power is no more to be committed to men
without discipline and restriction than alcohol.
H. G. WELLS, in *The Time Machine* (1905)

We want the facts to fit the preconceptions.
When they don't, it is easier to
ignore the facts than to change the preconceptions.
JESSAMYN WEST, in Introduction to *The Quaker Reader* (1962)

A religious awakening which does not
awaken the sleeper to love has roused him in vain.
JESSAMYN WEST, in Introduction to *The Quaker Reader* (1962)

A good cause has to be careful of the company it keeps.
REBECCA WEST, in *Sunday Times* (London; Aug. 23, 1942)

In a democracy...good will without competence
and competence without good will,
are both equivalent formulas for political disaster.
THEODORE H. WHITE, in *In Search of History* (1978)

We must always take sides.
Neutrality helps the oppressor, never the victim.
Silence encourages the tormentor, never the tormented.
ELIE WIESEL, in Nobel Prize Acceptance Speech (Dec. 10, 1986)

Some problems are just too complicated
for rational, logical solutions.
They admit of insights, not answers.
JEROME WIESNER, quoted in D. Lang, "Profiles: A Scientist's
Advice II," *The New Yorker* (Jan. 26, 1963)

When we say of people what we would not say to them,
we are either liars or cowards.

ELLA WHEELER WILCOX, in *An Ambitious Man* (1896)

To sin by silence when we should protest,
Makes cowards out of men.

ELLA WHEELER WILCOX, "Protest," in *Poems of Problems* (1914)

There is no sin except stupidity.

OSCAR WILDE, "The Critic as Artist," in *Intentions* (1891)

Misfortunes one can endure—
they come from outside, they are accidents.
But to suffer for one's own faults—
ah! There is the sting of life.

OSCAR WILDE, in *Lady Windermere's Fan* (1892)

An inarticulate President is like
a motorcycle motor installed in a Mack truck.

GEORGE F. WILL, in *Newsweek* (Apr. 20, 1975)

Will described Gerald Ford as "the most inarticulate President since
the invention of broadcasting," but there are many who believe
Donald Trump is even less articulate. Will, who ultimately left the
Republican Party after it was commandeered by Trump, considered
inarticulateness a fatal flaw in politics, writing: "Rhetorical skills are
not peripheral to the political enterprise, and they are among the most
important skills a person can bring to the Presidency." His essay also
included this generalization: "There never has been a great inarticulate President."

A politician's words reveal less about what he thinks
about his subject than what he thinks about his audience.

GEORGE F. WILL, quoted in Richard Reeves,
A Ford, Not a Lincoln (1975)

I think that deliberate, conscienceless mendacity,
the acceptance of falsehood and hypocrisy,
is the most dangerous of all sins.

TENNESSEE WILLIAMS, in interview with Don Ross,
New York Herald Tribune (Mar. 3, 1957)

In public affairs stupidity is more dangerous than knavery,
because [it is] harder to fight and dislodge.
If a man does not know enough to know
what the consequences are going to be to the country,
then he cannot govern the country in
a way that is for its benefit.

WOODROW WILSON, in *The New Freedom* (1913)

Wilson preceded the thought by writing: "I am very much more afraid
of the man who does a bad thing and does not know it is bad than of
the man who does a bad thing and knows it is bad."

A friend of mine says that every man
who takes office in Washington either grew or swelled.

WOODROW WILSON, in speech to the National Press
Club, Washington, DC (May 15, 1916)

Wilson continued: "And when I give a man an office, I watch him carefully to see whether he is swelling or growing." Wilson doesn't mention it, but his observation suggests that it is not only *appointees*, but *appointers* who either grow or swell.

Illusions are shattered by conflict with reality,
so no real happiness, no real wit, no real profundity
are tolerated where the illusion prevails.
VIRGINIA WOOLF, in *Orlando: A Biography* (1928)

If you do not tell the truth about yourself
you cannot tell it about other people.
VIRGINIA WOOLF, in *The Moment and Other Essays* (1952)

Ignorance is not bliss—it is oblivion.
Determined ignorance is the hastiest kind of oblivion.
PHILIP WYLIE, in *Generation of Vipers* (1942)

**You cannot trust
a man who
will sell himself
for a compliment.**

J. B. Yeats

The real leader serves truth,
not people.
J. B. YEATS, in *Letters to His Son, W. B. Yeats, and Others* (1946)

Yeats preceded the thought by writing: "People think of leaders as men devoted to service, and by service they mean that these men serve their followers."

You cannot trust a man
who will sell himself for a compliment.
J. B. YEATS, in *Letters to His Son, W. B. Yeats, and Others* (1946)

This is the concluding portion of a fuller thought that went this way: "Don't you think there is something touching about a vain man? He is all *one ache for your praise, would sell his soul for it* [italics mine]. Of course you cannot trust a man who will sell his soul for a compliment."

The best lack all conviction, while the worst
Are full of passionate intensity.
WILLIAM BUTLER YEATS, in "The Second Coming" (1921)

All empty souls tend to extreme opinion.
WILLIAM BUTLER YEATS, in *Autobiography of William Butler Yeats* (1938)

Why is it that right-wing bastards
always stand shoulder to shoulder in solidarity,
while liberals fall out among themselves?
YEVGENY YEVTUSHENKO, in *The Observer* (Dec. 15, 1991)

The press is too often a distorting mirror,
which deforms the people and events it represents,
making them seem bigger or smaller than they really are.

MARGUERITE YOURCENAR, in *With Open Eyes* (1980)

The man who has not the habit of reading
is imprisoned in his immediate world.

LIN YUTANG, in *The Importance of Living* (1937)

In a July 18, 2016 issue of *The New Yorker* (the month Trump won the Republican Party's nomination for president), Tony Schwartz, the ghostwriter of Trump's 1987 bestseller *The Art of the Deal*, told Jane Mayer: "I seriously doubt that Trump has ever read a book straight through in his adult life."

**Truth is on
the march
and nothing
can stop it.**

Émile Zola

Politics is the entertainment branch of industry.

FRANK ZAPPA, a signature saying, in *The
Real Frank Zappa Book* (1989)

Truth is on the march and nothing can stop it.

ÉMILE ZOLA, in *Le Figaro* (Nov. 25, 1897)

If you shut up truth and bury it under the ground,
it will but grow, and gather to itself such explosive power
that the day it bursts through
it will blow up everything in its way.

ÉMILE ZOLA, in an open letter in the French
newspaper *L'Aurore* (Jan. 13, 1898)

ACKNOWLEDGMENTS

My deepest gratitude goes to my wife, Katherine Robinson, a partner in every aspect of my life, including my book-writing efforts. I'm also deeply grateful to my agent, George Greenfield of *CreativeWell, Inc.*, for his decades-long support of my literary efforts.

This book would not have come into existence were if not for a generous contribution from an "angel investor" who arrived on the scene just as I was about to abandon the project. When the full story of my life is finally told, he will play a starring role.

This book also represents my first venture into the new world of "self-publishing," and the experience would have been completely overwhelming had I not found an able, experienced, and indispensable guide: David Wogahn of *Author Imprints*.

I would also like to express my deep appreciation to the many people who provided invaluable proofreading and editing assistance: Katie Barry, Jim Dekornfeld, Dr. Linnda Durré, Kelly Hardy, Rosalie Maggio, Nancy and George Meyer, Art Mills, and Carolanne Reynolds.

With this new book, I'm also beginning to venture into another new and (for me, at least) previously unexplored territory: the world of social media, particularly Instagram. At my stage of life, I must rely on younger, hipper, and more technologically sophisticated people—and I've been extremely fortunate to find Manon Wogahn, a talented graphic designer and Instagram specialist, to assist me in these new efforts.

Several thousand subscribers to my weekly e-newsletter ("Dr. Mardy's Quotes of the Week") have cheered me on for years and alerted me to many of the quotations that ultimately found their way into this book. There are far too many of them to list here, but my heartfelt thanks are extended to them all.

ABOUT THE AUTHOR

Dr. Mardy Grothe is a retired psychologist, management consultant, and platform speaker. After receiving his Ph.D. from Columbia University, he lived and worked in the Boston area until 2004, when he and his wife Katherine Robinson moved to North Carolina. Since 2011, they have lived in Southern Pines, NC, a vibrant community with an award-winning community newspaper, a thriving independent bookstore, and three wonderful public libraries.

A lifelong quotation collector, Grothe has published seven previous quotation anthologies. Known simply as "Dr. Mardy" to his many fans worldwide, he was hailed by Fred Shapiro, editor of *The Yale Book of Quotations* as "one of the most profound and popular quotation-book authors of all time." His books include:

> *Never Let a Fool Kiss You or a Kiss Fool You* (1999)
> *Oxymoronica* (2004)
> *Viva la Repartee* (2005)
> *I Never Metaphor I Didn't Like* (2008)
> *Ifferisms* (2009)
> *Neverisms* (2011)
> *Metaphors Be With You* (2016)

Grothe is also the creator of *Dr. Mardy's Dictionary of Metaphorical Quotations* (DMDMQ), the world's largest online database of metaphorical quotations, with over 40,000 quotations—all rigorously sourced—and organized into over 2,500 categories. About DMDMQ, Dr. Fuad Jaleel, a Wikipedia activist and administrator at Malayalam Wikiquote said, "Generations to come will scarce believe that ever in the history of collections of literary quotes has so much been done for so many by a single man."

CPSIA information can be obtained
at www.ICGtesting.com
Printed in the USA
LVHW030751210919
631813LV00007B/89